STILL STEAMING

A Guide to Britain's Standard Gauge Steam Railways 2007-2008

EDITOR
John Robinson

Eleventh Edition

ACKNOWLEDGEMENTS

We were greatly impressed by the friendly and cooperative manner of the staff and helpers of the railways which we selected to appear in this book, and wish to thank them all for the help they have given. In addition we wish to thank Bob Budd (cover design) and Michael Robinson (page layouts) for their help.

Although we believe that the information contained in this guide is accurate at the time of going to press, we, and the Railways and Museums itemised, are unable to accept liability for any loss, damage, distress or injury suffered as a result of any inaccuracies. Furthermore, we and the Railways are unable to guarantee operating and opening times which may always be subject to cancellation without notice.

If you feel we should include other locations or information in future editions, please let us know so that we may give them consideration. We would like to thank you for buying this guide and wish you 'Happy Steaming'!

John Robinson

EDITOR

Note: Further copies of Still Steaming, Little Puffers and Tiny Trains may be obtained, post free, from our address below or ordered on-line via our web site – www.stillsteaming.com

British Library Cataloguing in Publication Data
A catalogue record for this book is available from the British Library

ISBN-13: 978-1-86223-155-9

Copyright © 2007, MARKSMAN PUBLICATIONS. (01472 696226)
72 St. Peter's Avenue, Cleethorpes, N.E. Lincolnshire, DN35 8HU, England

Manufactured in the UK by LPPS Ltd, Wellingborough, NN8 3PJ

COVER PHOTOGRAPH

We are indebted to photographer Richard Barnett and the Foxfield Steam Railway for supplying the cover photo for this book.

This features Hunslet 0-6-0 saddle tank Austerity class 'Wimblebury' at Dilhorne Park Station.

CONTENTS

Acknowledgments 2
Contents 3-5
Friends of the National Railway Museum 6
National Railway Museum 7
Locomotion – The National Railway Museum at Shildon 8-9
Locator Map (North) 10
Locator Map (South) 11
Appleby Frodingham Railway Preservation Society 12
Avon Valley Railway 13
Barrow Hill Roundhouse Railway Centre 14
The Battlefield Line 15
Beamish – The North of England Open Air Museum 16
The Bluebell Railway 17
Bodmin & Wenford Railway 18
Bo'ness & Kinneil Railway 19
Bowes Railway 20
Bressingham Steam Museum 21
Bristol Harbour Railway 22
Buckinghamshire Railway Centre 23
Caledonian Railway 24
Chasewater Railway 25
Chinnor & Princes Risborough Railway 26
Cholsey & Wallingford Railway 27
Churnet Valley Railway 28

Colne Valley Railway 29
Crich Tramway Village 30
Darlington Railway Centre & Museum 31
The Dartmoor Railway 32
Dean Forest Railway 33
Derwent Valley Light Railway 34
Didcot Railway Centre 35
Downpatrick & County Down Railway 36
East Anglian Railway Museum 37
East Kent Light Railway 38
East Lancashire Railway 39
East Somerset Railway 40
Ecclesbourne Valley Railway 41
Elsecar Steam Railway 42
Embsay & Bolton Abbey Steam Railway 43
Epping Ongar Railway 44
Foxfield Steam Railway 45
Gloucestershire Warwickshire Railway 46
Great Central Railway 47
Gwili Railway 48
Hollycombe Steam Collection 49
Isle of Wight Steam Railway 50
Keighley & Worth Valley Railway 51
Kent & East Sussex Railway 52
Lakeside & Haverthwaite Railway 53
The Lavender Line 54
Lincolnshire Wolds Railway 55
Llangollen Railway 56
Mangapps Railway Museum 57
The Middleton Railway 58
Mid-Hants Railway (The Watercress Line) 59
Mid-Norfolk Railway 60
Mid-Suffolk Light Railway Museum 61
Midland Railway – Butterley 62
Nene Valley Railway 63
Northampton & Lamport Railway 64
North Norfolk Railway 65
North Tyneside Steam Railway 66
North Yorkshire Moors Railway 67
Nottingham Transport Heritage Centre 68
Paignton & Dartmouth Steam Railway 69

Pallot Steam Museum 70

Peak Rail PLC 71

Plym Valley Railway 72

Pontypool & Blaenavon Railway 73

Railway Preservation Society of Ireland 74

Ribble Steam Railway 75

Royal Deeside Railway 76

Rutland Railway Museum 77

Scottish Industrial Railway Centre 78

Severn Valley Railway 79

South Devon Railway 80

Spa Valley Railway 81

Steam – Museum of the Great Western Railway 82

Strathspey Steam Railway 83

Swanage Railway 84

Swansea Vale Railway 85

Swindon & Cricklade Railway 86

Tanfield Railway 87

Telford Steam Railway 88

Tyseley Locomotive Works 89

Vale of Glamorgan Railway 90

Weardale Railway 91

Wensleydale Railway 92

West Somerset Railway 93

Other railways under development 94-95

Advertisement – Tiny Trains and Little Puffers 96

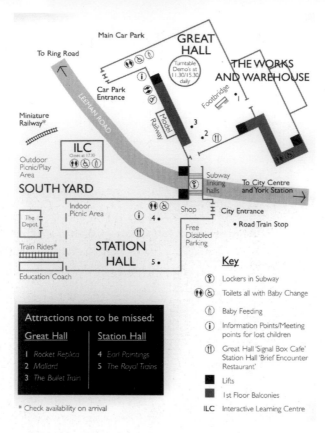

The map contains the following labels:

Main Car Park
To Ring Road
GREAT HALL
THE WORKS AND WAREHOUSE
Turntable Demo's at 11.30/15.30 daily
Car Park Entrance
Footbridge
LEEMAN ROAD
Miniature Railway*
Model Railway
3
2
ILC Opens at 17.30
Outdoor Picnic/Play Area
SOUTH YARD
Subway linking halls
To City Centre and York Station
The Depot
Indoor Picnic Area
4
Shop
City Entrance
Road Train Stop
Free Disabled Parking
Train Rides*
STATION HALL 5
Education Coach

Key

🔒 Lockers in Subway
🚻 Toilets all with Baby Change
🍼 Baby Feeding
ℹ️ Information Points/Meeting points for lost children
🍴 Great Hall 'Signal Box Cafe'
Station Hall 'Brief Encounter Restaurant'
■ Lifts
■ 1st Floor Balconies
ILC Interactive Learning Centre

Attractions not to be missed:

Great Hall	Station Hall
1 Rocket Replica	4 Earl Paintings
2 Mallard	5 The Royal Trains
3 The Bullet Train	

* Check availability on arrival

THE FRIENDS OF THE NATIONAL RAILWAY MUSEUM

This organisation was formed in 1977 to help conserve and operate railway exhibits that might otherwise have to wait many years before returning to public view. The organisation is run on a membership basis which imparts a number of privileges which include:

* the *NRM Review*, published quarterly, which keeps Friends in touch with events at the Museum, carries information about the National Collection locomotives, features articles of general railway interest and includes authorative reviews of videos and books.

* opportunities to work as a volunteer in the Museum.

* invitations to FNRM members meetings in York and London.

MEMBERSHIP DETAILS – Normal membership is valid for 12 months from date of registration.

Category	Rate
Ordinary	£20.00
Unwaged	£15.00
Junior (Under 18)	£10.00
Family/Couple	£30.00
Retired Couple	£22.50
Group	£35.00
Life (below 60)	£300.00
Life (60 and over)	£225.00
Life (retired couple)	£350.00
Life (family)	£450.00

Apply for membership to:

FNRM
National Railway Museum
Leeman Road
York
YO26 4XJ

Telephone (01904) 636874
e-mail fnrm@nmsi.ac.uk

Family Membership – is for a maximum of four persons, two or three of whom are under 18 years of age, residing at the same address

Retired Couple Membership – is for two persons aged 60 or over and not in employment.

National Railway Museum

Address: National Railway Museum, Leeman Road, York   YO26 4XJ
Telephone Nº: 0870 421-4001
Fax Nº: (01904) 611112
E-mail: nrm@nrm.org.uk
Web site: www.nrm.org.uk

Year Formed: 1975
Location of Line: York
Length of Line: Short demonstration line
Nº of Steam Locos: 79
Nº of Other Locos: 37
Approx Nº of Visitors P.A.: 800,000

GENERAL INFORMATION

Nearest Mainline Station: York (¼ mile)
Nearest Bus Station: York (¼ mile)
Car Parking: On site car park (£7.00 per day)
Coach Parking: On site – free to pre-booked groups
Souvenir Shop(s): Yes
Food & Drinks: Yes

SPECIAL INFORMATION

The Museum is the largest of its kind in the world, housing the Nation's collection of locomotives, carriages, uniforms, posters and an extensive photographic archive. Special events and exhibitions run throughout the year. The Museum is the home of the Mallard – the fastest steam locomotive in the world and Shinkansen, the only Bullet train outside of Japan.

OPERATING INFORMATION

Opening Times: Open daily 10.00am to 6.00pm (closed on 24th, 25th and 26th of December)
Steam Working: School holidays – please phone to confirm details
Prices: Free admission for all (excludes some Special events)
Phone (01904) 686263 for further details.

Detailed Directions by Car:
The Museum is located in the centre of York, just behind the Railway Station. It is clearly signposted from all approaches to York.

Shildon is one of the world's oldest railway towns and was selected by the National Railway Museum as a site for Locomotion, the first national museum to be built in the North East. The new building houses the reserve collection of historically important railway vehicles and these are now accessible to the public for the first time.

Shildon was home to the Timothy Hackworth Museum with its workshops and historic buildings and the incorporation of these with the new Locomotion museum creates an exciting opportunity to discover the significance of Shildon in railway history.

The replica Sans Pareil locomotive pictured below gives rides during the Summer School Holidays and on other special event days.

LOCOMOTION – THE NATIONAL RAILWAY MUSEUM AT SHILDON

Address: Locomotion, Shildon, County Durham DL14 1PQ **Telephone Nº:** (01388) 777999 **Fax Nº:** (01388) 771448 **Year Formed:** 2004 **Location:** Shildon, County Durham	**Length of Line:** Over ½ mile **Nº of Steam Locos:** 60 locomotives and other rail vehicles **Approx Nº of Visitors P.A.:** 60,000+ **Gauge:** Standard **Web site:** www.locomotion.uk.com

GENERAL INFORMATION

Nearest Mainline Station: Shildon (adjacent)
Nearest Bus Station: Durham
Car Parking: Available on site
Coach Parking: Available on site
Souvenir Shop(s): Yes
Food & Drinks: Yes

SPECIAL INFORMATION

This extensive site is the first regional branch of the National Railway Museum and houses vehicles from the National Collection in a purpose-built 6,000 square-foot building.

OPERATING INFORMATION

Opening Times: Daily from 27th May 2007 to 30th September 2007 – 10.00am to 5.00pm. Also open from Wednesday to Sunday during the Winter season – 1st October to 1st April from 10.00am to 4.00pm although the Museum is closed over the Christmas and New Year Holiday period.
Steam Working: During the Summer School Holidays and on special event days – please phone to confirm details.
Prices: Free admission for all.

Detailed Directions by Car:
From All Parts: Exit the A1(M) at Junction 58 and take the A68 and the A6072 to Shildon. Follow the Brown tourist signs to Locomotion which is situated ¼ mile to the south-east of the Town Centre.

RAILWAY LOCATOR MAP

The numbers shown on this map relate to the page numbers for each railway. Pages 3-5 contain an alphabetical listing of the railways featured in this guide. Please note that the markers on this map show the approximate location only.

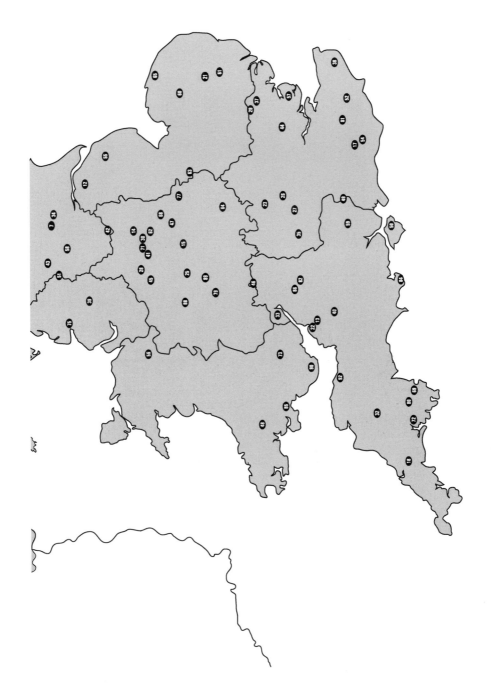

APPLEBY FRODINGHAM RAILWAY

Address: Appleby Frodingham Railway Preservation Society, P.O. Box 44, Brigg, North Lincolnshire DN20 8DW	**Length of Line**: 18 miles of track
	Nº of Steam Locos: 3
	Nº of Other Locos: 2
Telephone Nº: (01652) 656661	**Nº of Members**: 60
Year Formed: 1990	**Annual Membership Fee**: –
Location of Line: Corus Steelworks, Scunthorpe	**Gauge**: Standard
	Web site: www.afrps.co.uk

GENERAL INFORMATION

Nearest Mainline Station: Scunthorpe (2 miles)
Nearest Bus Station: Scunthorpe (2 miles)
Car Parking: Large free car park at the site
Coach Parking: At the site
Souvenir Shop(s): Yes – at the Loco Shed
Food & Drinks: Drinks/snacks served on train trips

SPECIAL INFORMATION

A selection of Rail tours and Brake Van tours are operated over a distance of 7 to 18 miles of the steelworks internal railway system.

OPERATING INFORMATION

Opening Times: Selected weekends throughout the year which must be pre-booked via (01652) 657053 or e-mail – bookings@afrps.co.uk
Private Hire of a train is now available for parties and anniveraries with use of the Lounge coach.
Steam Working: See above
Prices: Free – but donations are accepted
Please note that children cannot be carried on Brake van tours due to the open verandahs.

Detailed Directions by Car:
Exit the M180 at Junction 3 onto the M181, at the end turn right onto the A18. Take the 3rd exit at the roundabout (still on the A18) and turn left onto Ashby Road at the next roundabout. At the following roundabout turn right into Rowland Road and at the end of the road turn right then left into Entrance E. Car parking is available on the left and the path to the station is on the right.

AVON VALLEY RAILWAY

Address: Bitton Station, Bath Road, Bitton, Bristol BS30 6HD
Telephone Nº: (0117) 932-7296
Year Formed: 1973
Location of Line: Midway between Bristol and Bath on A431
Length of Line: 3 miles

Nº of Steam Locos: 6
Nº of Other Locos: 3
Nº of Members: Approximately 600
Annual Membership Fee: £15.00
Approx Nº of Visitors P.A.: 80,000
Gauge: Standard
Web site: www.avonvalleyrailway.org

GENERAL INFO

Nearest Mainline Station: Keynsham (1½ miles)
Nearest Bus Station: Bristol or Bath (7 miles)
Car Parking: Available at Bitton Station
Coach Parking: Available at Bitton Station
Souvenir Shop(s): Yes
Food & Drinks: Yes

SPECIAL INFO

The line has been extended through the scenic Avon Valley towards Bath and a new platform is now open linking with boat trips along the River Avon.

OPERATING INFO

Opening Times: Every Sunday and some Saturdays from Easter to October and on weekends during December. Also Bank Holiday Mondays and Tuesdays to Thursdays during School Holidays. Also open for Santa Specials over Christmas. Open 10.30am to 5.00pm.
Steam Working: 11.00am to 4.00pm
Prices: Adult £5.50
 Child £4.00
 Family Tickets £15.00
 Senior Citizens £4.50

Detailed Directions by Car:
From All Parts: Exit the M4 at Junction 18. Follow the A46 towards Bath and at the junction with the A420 turn right towards Bristol. At Bridge Yate turn left onto the A4175 and continue until you reach the A431. Turn right and Bitton Station is 100 yards on the right.

BARROW HILL ROUNDHOUSE RAILWAY CENTRE

Address: Barrow Hill Roundhouse, Campbell Drive, Barrow Hill, Staveley, Chesterfield   S43 2PR
Telephone Nº: (01246) 472450
Year Formed: 1998
Location: Staveley, near Chesterfield
Length of Line: ¾ mile

Nº of Steam Locos: 9
Nº of Other Locos: Over 40
Nº of Members: Approximately 400
Annual Membership Fee: £15.00 (Adult)
Approx Nº of Visitors P.A.: 30,000
Gauge: Standard
Web site: www.barrowhill.org.uk

GENERAL INFORMATION

Nearest Mainline Station:
Chesterfield (3½ miles)
Nearest Bus Station:
Chesterfield (3 miles)
Car Parking: Space available for 200 cars
Coach Parking: Available
Souvenir Shop(s): Yes
Food & Drinks: Yes – buffet

SPECIAL INFORMATION

Britain's last remaining operational Railway roundhouse provides storage and repair facilities for standard gauge steam, diesel and electric locomotives.

OPERATING INFORMATION

Opening Times: Open at weekends throughout the year from 10.00am to 4.30pm (for static viewing).
Steam Working: Special open days only – Real Ale Festival on 18th & 19th May; Steam Gala on 10th & 11th November (Diesel Gala on 14th & 15th July though with no steaming); Santa Steam Trains on 16th and 23rd December. Please phone for further details or check the railway's web site.
Prices: Please phone for prices
Note: Driver training courses are available – please phone for further details.

Detailed Directions by Car:
Exit the M1 at Junction 30 and take the A619 to Staveley (about 3½ miles). Pass through Staveley, turn right at Troughbrook onto 'Works Road'. Continue along for ¾ mile, pass under the railway bridge and take the turn immediately on the right. Turn left onto Campbell Drive and the Roundhouse is behind Acorn Van Hire. The railway is signposted with Brown Tourist signs.

THE BATTLEFIELD LINE

Address: The Battlefield Line,
Shackerstone Station, Shackerstone,
Warwickshire   CV13 6NW
Telephone Nº: (01827) 880754
Year Formed: 1968
Location of Line: North West of Market
Bosworth
Length of Line: 5 miles

Nº of Steam Locos: 5
Nº of Other Locos: 20
Nº of Members: 500 approximately
Annual Membership Fee: £15.00 Adult;
£25.00 Family
Approx Nº of Visitors P.A.: 50,000
Gauge: Standard
Web site: www.battlefield-line-railway.co.uk

GENERAL INFORMATION

Nearest Mainline Station: Nuneaton (9 miles)
Nearest Bus Station: Nuneaton & Hinckley (9 miles)
Car Parking: Ample free parking available
Coach Parking: Can cater for coach parties
Souvenir Shop(s): Yes
Food & Drinks: Yes – Station Buffet

SPECIAL INFORMATION

Travel from the Grade II listed Shackerstone Station
through the beautiful Leicestershire countryside
with views of the adjoining Ashby Canal. Arrive at
the award-winning Shenton Station and explore
Bosworth Battlefield (1485) before making the
return journey.

OPERATING INFORMATION

Operating Info: Weekends and Bank Holidays from
Easter to October and Santa Specials on weekends
from 25th November to Christmas Eve. Also open
on Wednesday afternoons in July and August. Please
telephone for further details.
Opening Times: 11.00am to 5.00pm
Steam Working: From 11.15am to 4.15pm during
high season and Sundays.
Prices: Adult Return £7.00
       Child Return £4.00 (ages 5-15 years)
       O.A.P. Return £5.00
       Family Ticket £20.00
       (2 adults and 2 children)

Detailed Directions by Car:
Follow the brown tourist signs from the A444 or A447 heading towards the market town of Market Bosworth.
Continue towards the villages of Congerstone & Shackerstone and finally to Shackerstone Station. Access is only
available via the Old Trackbed.

BEAMISH – THE NORTH OF ENGLAND OPEN AIR MUSEUM

Address: Beamish North of England Open Air Museum, Co. Durham   DH9 0RG
Telephone Nº: (0191) 370-4000
Year Formed: 1970
Length of Line: ½ mile

Nº of Steam Locos: 10
Nº of Other Locos: 2
N.B.: Not all Locos are on display
Approx Nº of Visitors P.A.: 320,000
Web site: www.beamish.org.uk

GENERAL INFORMATION

Nearest Mainline Station: Newcastle Central (8 miles);   Durham City (12 miles)
Nearest Bus Station: Durham (12 miles), Newcastle (8 miles)
Car Parking: Free parking for 2,000 cars
Coach Parking: Free parking for 40 coaches
Souvenir Shop(s): Yes
Food & Drinks: Yes – self service tea room, licensed period Public House and a Coffee shop.

SPECIAL INFORMATION

A replica of William Hedley's famous 1813 locomotive "Puffing Billy" steams on the Pockerley Waggonway at Beamish alongside replicas of Locomotion and the Steam Elephant.

OPERATING INFORMATION

Opening Times: Open all year round: from 10.00am to 4.00pm in the Winter (November to March). Closed on Mondays and Fridays in the Winter. Open from 10.00am to 5.00pm during the Summer (April to October). Check for Christmas opening times.
N.B. Winter visits are centred on the Town and Tramway only. Other areas are closed and admission prices are reduced.
Allow 4-5 hours for a Summer visit and two hours in the Winter.
Steam Working: Daily during the Summer
Prices:
Adult £16.00 in Summer; £6.00 in Winter
Child £10.00 in Summer; £6.00 in Winter
O.A.P. £12.50 in Summer; £6.00 in Winter
Children under 5 are admitted free.
Special Family Tickets are available.

Detailed Directions by Car:
From North & South: Follow the A1(M) to Junction 63 (Chester-le-street) and then take A693 for 4 miles towards Stanley; From North-West: Take the A68 south to Castleside near Consett and follow the signs on the A692 and A693 via Stanley.

THE BLUEBELL RAILWAY

Address: The Bluebell Railway, Sheffield Park Station, Nr. Uckfield, East Sussex, TN22 3QL
Telephone Nº: (01825) 720800
Information Line: (01825) 720825
Year Formed: 1959
Location of Line: Nr. Uckfield, E. Sussex
Length of Line: 9 miles

Nº of Steam Locos: Over 30 with up to 3 in operation on any given day
Nº of Other Locos: –
Nº of Members: 8,000
Annual Membership Fee: £17.00 Adult
Approx Nº of Visitors P.A.: 175,000
Gauge: Standard
Web site: www.bluebell-railway.co.uk

GENERAL INFORMATION

Nearest Mainline Station: East Grinstead (2 miles) with a bus connection
Nearest Bus Station: East Grinstead
Car Parking: Parking at Sheffield Park and Horsted Keynes Stations.
Coach Parking: Sheffield Park is best
Souvenir Shop(s): Yes
Food & Drinks: Yes – buffets and licensed bars & restaurant

SPECIAL INFORMATION

The Railway runs 'Golden Arrow' dining trains on Saturday evenings and Sunday lunchtimes. There is also a museum and model railway at Sheffield Park Station.

OPERATING INFORMATION

Opening Times: Open every weekend throughout the year and also daily from April to October inclusive. Also open during School holidays and for Santa Specials during December. Open from approximately 10.30am to 5.30pm
Steam Working: As above
Prices: Adult Return £9.80
Child Return £4.90
Family Return £28.00 (2 adult + 3 child)

Detailed Directions by Car:
Sheffield Park Station is situated on the A275 Wych Cross to Lewes road. Horsted Keynes Station is signposted from the B2028 Lingfield to Haywards Heath road.

Bodmin & Wenford Railway

Address: Bodmin General Station, Losthwithiel Road, Bodmin, Cornwall PL31 1AQ	**Nº of Steam Locos:** 10
	Nº of Other Locos: 9
	Nº of Members: 850
Telephone Nº: (0845) 1259678	**Annual Membership Fee:** £12.00
Year Formed: 1984	**Approx Nº of Visitors P.A.:** 51,500
Location of Line: Bodmin Parkway Station to Bodmin General & Boscarne Junction.	**Gauge:** Standard
	Web: www.bodminandwenfordrailway.co.uk
Length of Line: 6½ miles	

GENERAL INFORMATION

Nearest Mainline Station: Bodmin Parkway (cross platform interchange with the Bodmin & Wenford Railway)
Car Parking: Free parking at site
Coach Parking: Free parking at site
Souvenir Shop(s): Yes
Food & Drinks: Yes

SPECIAL INFORMATION

The Railway has steep gradients and there are two different branches to choose from Bodmin General. Through tickets to "Bodmin & Wenford Railway" are available from all Mainline stations.

OPERATING INFORMATION

Opening Times: Daily from 26th May to the end of September. Also daily during Easter week. Open other selected dates from March to May + October and also for Santa Specials in December. Open from 10.00am to 5.00pm but also during certain evenings in the Summer.
Steam Working: Usually trains are steam-hauled except for most Saturdays when Diesels are used.
Prices: Adult Return £7.50 to £10.00
Child Return £4.00 to £6.00
Family Return £21.50 to £28.00
(2 adults + 2 children)

Detailed Directions by Car:
From the A30/A38 follow the signs to Bodmin Town Centre then follow the brown tourist signs to the Steam Railway on the B3268 Losthwithiel Road.

BO'NESS & KINNEIL RAILWAY

Address: Bo'ness Station, Union Street, Bo'ness, West Lothian   EH51 9AQ
Telephone No: (01506) 822298
Year Opened: 1981
Location of Line: Bo'ness to Birkhill
Length of Line: 3½ miles

No of Steam Locos: 26
No of Other Locos: 25
No of Members: 1,300
Annual Membership Fee: £17.00
Approx No of Visitors P.A.: 60,000
Gauge: Standard
Web site: www.srps.org.uk

GENERAL INFORMATION

Nearest Mainline Station: Linlithgow (3 miles)
Nearest Bus Station: Bo'ness (¼ mile)
Car Parking: Free parking at Bo'ness and Birkhill Stations
Coach Parking: Free parking at Bo'ness Station
Souvenir Shop(s): Yes
Food & Drinks: Yes

SPECIAL INFORMATION

The Scottish Railway Exhibition is situated at Bo'ness and conducted tours are also available of the caverns of Birkhill Mine. The Bo'ness Railway is operated by volunteers of the Scottish Railway Preservation Society.

OPERATING INFORMATION

Opening Times: Open on weekends from 31st March to 28th October. Also open daily from 30th June to 26th August with diesels only running on Mondays in July.
Steam Working: The first train leaves at 11.00am and is steam-hauled as are all trains during the day. The last train leaves at 4.15pm and is diesel-hauled.
Prices: Adult Return £5.00   Child Return £2.50
Family Return £13.00   Concession Return £4.00
N.B. Group discounts are also available – please phone for further details. Also, special fares and timetables apply for special events.

Detailed Directions by Car:
From Edinburgh: Take the M9 and exit at Junction 3. Then take the A904 to Bo'ness; From Glasgow: Take the M80 to M876 and then M9 (South). Exit at Junction 5 and take A904 to Bo'ness; From the North: Take M9 (South), exit at Junction 5, then take A904 to Bo'ness; From Fife: Leave the A90 after the Forth Bridge, then take A904 to Bo'ness.

BOWES RAILWAY

Address: Bowes Railway, Springwell Village, Gateshead, Tyne & Wear NE9 7QJ	**N° of Steam Locos**: 2
Telephone N°: (0191) 416-1847	**N° of Other Locos**: 4
Year Formed: 1976	**N° of Members**: Approximately 70
Location of Line: Springwell Village	**Annual Membership Fee**: £12.00
Length of Line: 1¼ miles	**Approx N° of Visitors P.A.**: 5,000
	Gauge: Standard
	Web site: www.bowesrailway.co.uk

GENERAL INFORMATION

Nearest Mainline Station: Newcastle Central (3 miles)
Nearest Bus Station: Gateshead Interchange (2 miles)
Car Parking: Free parking at site
Coach Parking: Free parking at site
Souvenir Shop(s): Yes
Food & Drinks: Yes

SPECIAL INFORMATION

Designed by George Stephenson and opened in 1826, the Railway is a scheduled Ancient Monument which operates unique preserved standard gauge rope-hauled inclines and steam hauled passenger trains.

OPERATING INFORMATION

Opening Times: The Springwell site is open for static viewing (no charges) on weekdays and some Saturdays throughout the year – 10.00am to 3.00pm.
Steam Working: 12th and 13th May, 3rd June, 8th September, 14th October and Santa Specials on 1st, 2nd, 8th and 9th of December (please book early for these to avoid disappointment). A Rope-Haulage weekend is to be held on 21st and 22nd July.
Prices: No charges for visting but admission fees are charged for special events. Please contact the railway or check the web site for further details.

Detailed Directions by Car:
From A1 (Northbound): Follow the A194(M) to the Tyne Tunnel and turn left at the sign for Springwell; From A1 (Southbound): Take the turn off left for the B1288 to Springwell and Wrekenton.

BRESSINGHAM STEAM EXPERIENCE

Address: Bressingham Steam Museum, Bressingham, Diss, Norfolk   IP22 2AB
Telephone Nº: (01379) 686900
Year Formed: Mid 1950's
Location of Line: Bressingham, Near Diss
Length of Line: 5 miles in total (3 lines)

Nº of Steam Locos: Many Steam locos
Nº of Members: 70 volunteers
Annual Membership Fee: –
Approx Nº of Visitors P.A.: 80,000+
Gauge: Standard, 2 foot, 10¼ inches and 15 inches
Web site: www.bressingham.co.uk

GENERAL INFORMATION

Nearest Mainline Station: Diss (2½ miles)
Nearest Bus Station: Bressingham (1¼ miles)
Car Parking: Free parking for 400 cars available
Coach Parking: Free parking for 30 coaches
Souvenir Shop(s): Yes
Food & Drinks: Yes

SPECIAL INFORMATION

In addition to Steam locomotives, Bressingham has a large selection of steam traction engines, fixed steam engines and also the National Dad's Army Museum, two extensive gardens and a water garden centre.

OPERATING INFORMATION

Opening Times: Daily from 24th March to the 28th October 10.30am to 5.00pm. Open until 5.30pm in June, July and August.
Steam Working: Almost every operating day except for most Mondays & Tuesdays in March, April, May, June, July, September and October. Phone for further details.
Prices: Adult £9.00 (non-Steam) £12.00 (Steam)
        Child £6.00 (non-Steam) £8.00 (Steam)
        Family £25 (non-Steam) £35.00 (Steam)
        Seniors £8 (non-Steam) £10.50 (Steam)

Detailed Directions by Car:
From All Parts: Take the A11 to Thetford and then follow the A1066 towards Diss for Bressingham. The Museum is signposted by the brown tourist signs.

BRISTOL HARBOUR RAILWAY

Address: Bristol Industrial Museum, Princes Wharf, City Docks, Bristol, BS1 4RN	**Length of Line**: 1½ miles
	N° of Steam Locos: 2
	N° of Other Locos: 1
Telephone N°: (0117) 922-3571	**N° of Members**: –
Year Formed: 1978	**Annual Membership Fee**: –
Location of Line: South side of the Floating Harbour	**Approx N° of Visitors P.A.**: 70,000
	Gauge: Standard

GENERAL INFORMATION

Nearest Mainline Station: Bristol Temple Meads (1 mile)
Nearest Bus Station: City Centre (½ mile)
Car Parking: Parking available at site
Coach Parking: Drop off and Pick up only
Souvenir Shop(s): Yes
Food & Drinks: Cafes available near the Railway

SPECIAL INFORMATION

Although the Museum is current closed for redevelopment, the railway will continue to operate during 2007 on a limited basis.

OPERATING INFORMATION

Opening Times: Bank Holidays and also on 1st, 28th & 29th July and the 8th September. Please phone for confirmation of these dates.
Steam Working: Please contact the railway for details.
Prices: Return £1.00 – £2.00 (Depends on length
Single £0.50 – £1.00 of the journey)
Note: Children under the age of 6 travel for free.

Detailed Directions by Car:
From All Parts: Follow signs to Bristol City Centre and then the Brown Tourist signs for the Museum. A good landmark to look out for are the 4 huge quayside cranes.

BUCKINGHAMSHIRE RAILWAY CENTRE

Address: Quainton Road Station, Quainton, Aylesbury, Bucks. HP22 4BY	**Nº of Steam Locos:** 30
Telephone Nº: (01296) 655720	**Nº of Other Locos:** 6
Year Formed: 1969	**Nº of Members:** 1,000
Location of Line: At Quainton on the old Metropolitan/Great Central Line	**Annual Membership Fee:** £15.00
	Approx Nº of Visitors P.A.: 40,000
	Gauge: Standard (also a Miniature line)
Length of Line: 2 × ½ mile demo tracks	**Recorded Info. Line:** (01296) 655450

GENERAL INFORMATION

Nearest Mainline Station: Aylesbury (6 miles)
Nearest Bus Station: Aylesbury
Car Parking: Free parking for 500 cars available
Coach Parking: Free parking for 10 coaches
Souvenir Shop(s): Yes
Food & Drinks: Yes

SPECIAL INFORMATION

In addition to a large collection of locomotives and carriages, the Centre has an extensive ½ mile outdoor miniature railway system operated by the Vale of Aylesbury Model Engineering Society.

Web site: www.bucksrailcentre.org

OPERATING INFORMATION

Opening Times: Wednesday to Sunday and Bank Holidays from April to October. Open from 10.30am to 4.30pm.
Steam Working: Sundays and Bank Holidays from April to October and also on Wednesdays during the School holidays.
Prices: Adult £5.00 – £8.00
Child £2.50 – £4.50
(Under 5's travel free of charge)
Senior Citizen £4.00 – £6.00
Family £21.00 – £23.00
(2 adults + up to 4 children)
Note: Rides on the Miniature Railway cost 70p

Detailed Directions by Car:
The Buckinghamshire Railway Centre is signposted off the A41 Aylesbury to Bicester Road at Waddesdon and off the A413 Buckingham to Aylesbury road at Whitchurch. Junctions 7, 8 and 9 of the M40 are all close by.

CALEDONIAN RAILWAY

Address: The Station, 2 Park Road, Brechin, Angus DD9 7AF
Telephone Nº: (01561) 377760
Year Formed: 1979
Location of Line: From Brechin to the Bridge of Dun
Length of Line: 4 miles

Nº of Steam Locos: 10
Nº of Other Locos: 12
Nº of Members: 250
Annual Membership Fee: Adult £12.00; Family £15.00; OAP/Junior £5.00
Approx Nº of Visitors P.A.: 12,000
Gauge: Standard
Web site: www.caledonianrailway.co.uk

GENERAL INFORMATION

Nearest Mainline Station: Montrose (4½ miles)
Nearest Bus Station: Brechin (200 yards)
Car Parking: Ample free parking at both Stations
Coach Parking: Free parking at both Stations
Souvenir Shop(s): Yes
Food & Drinks: Light refreshments are available

SPECIAL INFORMATION

Brechin Station is the only original Terminus station in preservation.

OPERATING INFORMATION

Opening Times: Easter specials, Christmas specials in December and every Sunday from 27th May to 2nd September. Also open on 21st and 28th July, 11th and 18th August. Contact the railway for details of other Special Events throughout the year.
Steam Working: Steam service on every Sunday.
Prices: Adult Return £5.00
 Child Return £3.00
 Senior Citizen Return £4.00
 Family Return £16.00 (2 adult + 3 child)
Group discounts are available if booked in advance.

Detailed Directions by Car:
From South: For Brechin Station, leave the A90 at the Brechin turn-off and go straight through the Town Centre. Pass the Northern Hotel, take the 2nd exit at the mini-roundabout then it is 150 yards to Park Road/St. Ninian Square; From North: For Brechin Station, leave the A90 at the Brechin turn-off and go straight through Trinity Village. Turn left at the mini-roundabout, it is then 250 yards to Park Road/St. Ninian Square. Bridge of Dun is situated half way between Brechin and Montrose. (Follow tourist signs).

CHASEWATER RAILWAY

Address: Chasewater Country Park, Pool Road, Near Brownhills, Staffs, WS8 7NL	**Nº of Steam Locos**: 9
	Nº of Other Locos: 14
	Nº of Members: 700
Telephone Nº: (01543) 452623	**Annual Membership Fee**: Adult £15.00;
Year Re-formed: 1985	Family £20.00; Concessions £10.00
Location of Line: Chasewater Country Park, Brownhills, near Walsall	**Approx Nº of Visitors P.A.**: 36,500
	Gauge: Standard
Length of Line: 2 miles	**Web site**: www.chaserail.com

GENERAL INFORMATION

Nearest Mainline Station: Walsall or Birmingham (both approximately 8 miles)
Nearest Bus Station: Walsall or Birmingham
Car Parking: Free parking in Chasewater Park
Coach Parking: Free parking in Chasewater Park
Souvenir Shop(s): Yes
Food & Drinks: Yes

SPECIAL INFORMATION

Chasewater Railway is based on the Cannock Chase & Wolverhampton Railway opened in 1856. The railway passed into the hands of the National Coal Board which then ceased using the line in 1965. An extension to Chasetown and a new station at Chasewater Heaths is now open as is a new Heritage Centre at Brownhills West.

OPERATING INFORMATION

Opening Times: Sundays and Bank Holiday Mondays throughout the year plus most Saturdays from June to September and Wednesdays from 20th June to 29th August. Also Santa Specials in December. A regular service runs from 10.30am on operating days.
Steam Working: Please phone for details.
Prices: Adult Return £2.95
Child Return £1.95
Family Return £7.45
All tickets offer unlimited rides on the day of issue.

Detailed Directions by Car:
Chasewater Country Park is situated in Brownhills off the A5 southbound near the junction of the A5 with the A452 Chester Road. Follow the Brown tourist signs on the A5 for the Country Park.

CHINNOR & PRINCES RISBOROUGH RAILWAY

Address: Station Road, Chinnor, Oxon	**Nº of Steam Locos:** 1
Telephone Nº: (01844) 353535 (timetable)	**Nº of Other Locos:** 3
Year Formed: 1989	**Nº of Members:** 1,000
Location of Line: The Icknield Line, Chinnor	**Annual Membership Fee:** Adult £13.00; Family £20.00; Child £5.00; OAP £8.00
Length of Line: 3½ miles	**Approx Nº of Visitors P.A.:** 15,000
Gauge: Standard	**Web Site:** www.cprra.co.uk

Photo courtesy of Peter Harris

GENERAL INFORMATION

Nearest Mainline Station: Princes Risborough (4 miles)
Nearest Bus Station: High Wycombe (10 miles)
Car Parking: Free parking at site
Coach Parking: Prior arrangement preferred but not necessary
Souvenir Shop(s): Yes
Food & Drinks: Soft drinks and light snacks in Station Buffet. Buffet usually available on trains.

SPECIAL INFORMATION

The Chinnor & Princes Risborough Railway operates the remaining 3½ mile section of the former GWR Watlington Branch from Chinnor to Thame Junction.

OPERATING INFORMATION

Opening Times: Sundays from mid-March to October and also in December and Saturdays during July and August.
Steam Working: Operates from 10.00am to 5.00pm on Sundays.
Prices: Adult £7.50
Child £3.75
Family £19.50 (2 adults + 2 children)
Senior Citizen £6.50

Detailed Directions by Car:
From All Parts: The railway at Chinnor is situated in Station Road just off the B4009. Junction 6 of the M40 is 4 miles away and Princes Risborough 4 miles further along the B4009. Once in Chinnor follow the brown Tourist signs to the railway.

CHOLSEY & WALLINGFORD RAILWAY

Address: Wallingford Station,
5 Hithercroft Road, Wallingford, Oxon,
OX10 9GQ
Telephone Nº: (01491) 835067 (24hr info)
Year Formed: 1981
Location of Line: Wallingford, Oxon.
Length of Line: 2½ miles

Nº of Steam Locos: 1 (+ visiting Locos)
Nº of Other Locos: 4
Nº of Members: 250
Annual Membership Fee: £12.50
Approx Nº of Visitors P.A.: 6,500
Gauge: Standard
Web: www.cholsey-wallingford-railway.com

GENERAL INFORMATION

Nearest Mainline Station: Joint station at Cholsey
Nearest Bus Station: Wallingford (¼ mile)
Car Parking: Off road parking available
Coach Parking: Off road parking available
Souvenir Shop(s): Yes
Food & Drinks: Yes

SPECIAL INFORMATION

The Wallingford branch was originally intended as a through line to Princes Risborough, via Watlington, but became the first standard gauge branch of Brunel's broad-gauge London to Bristol line.

OPERATING INFORMATION

Opening Times: Selected weekends from Easter until Christmas – please phone for further details.
Steam Working: Approximately 11.00am to 4.30pm
Prices: Adult Return £6.00
Child Return £4.00
Concessionary Return £4.50
Family Return £15.50 (2 adult + 3 child)
Prices: Prices are subject to change for Engine visits and other special events.

Detailed Directions by Car:
From All Parts: Exit from the A34 at the Milton Interchange (between E. Ilsley and Abingdon). Follow signs to Didcot and Wallingford (A4130). Take Wallingford bypass, then turn left at the first roundabout (signposted Hithercroft Road). The Station is then ½ mile on the right.

CHURNET VALLEY RAILWAY

Address: The Railway Station, Cheddleton, Leek, Staffs. ST13 7EE	**N° of Steam Locos:** 2
Telephone N°: (01538) 360522	**N° of Other Locos:** 3
Year Formed: 1978	**N° of Members:** –
Location of Line: Cheddleton to Froghall	**Annual Membership Fee:** £14.00
Length of Line: 5½ miles	**Approx N° of Visitors P.A.:** 65,000
	Gauge: Standard
	Web site: www.churnetvalleyrailway.co.uk

GENERAL INFORMATION

Nearest Mainline Station: Stoke-on-Trent (12 miles)
Nearest Bus Station: Leek (5 miles)
Car Parking: Parking available on site
Coach Parking: Restricted space – please book in advance
Souvenir Shop(s): Yes
Food & Drinks: Yes

SPECIAL INFORMATION

Cheddleton Station is a Grade II listed building, Consall is a sleepy halt with Victorian charm, whereas Kingsley & Froghall has been rebuilt in NSR style and includes disabled facilities and a tearoom.

OPERATING INFORMATION

Opening Times: Trains run from 10.30am on most operating days or from 10.00am on Bank Holidays and Special Event days.
Steam Working: Sundays from March to October, Saturdays from June to September, Wednesdays in July and August and all Bank Holiday Mondays. Also various other special events throughout the year.
Prices: Please telephone (01538) 360522 for details.

Detailed Directions by Car:
From All Parts: Take the M6 to Stoke-on-Trent and follow trunk roads to Leek. Cheddleton Station is just off the A520 Leek to Stone road. Kingsley & Froghall Station is just off the A52 Ashbourne Road.

COLNE VALLEY RAILWAY

Address: Castle Hedingham Station, Yeldham Road, Castle Hedingham, Essex, CO9 3DZ	**N° of Steam Locos**: 10
	N° of Other Locos: 11
	N° of Members: 280
Telephone N°: (01787) 461174	**Annual Membership Fee**: £11.00
Year Formed: 1974	**Approx N° of Visitors P.A.**: 45,000
Location of Line: On A1017, 7 miles north-west of Braintree	**Gauge**: Standard
	Web Site: www.colnevalleyrailway.co.uk
Length of Line: Approximately 1 mile	

GENERAL INFORMATION

Nearest Mainline Station: Braintree (7 miles)
Nearest Bus Station: Hedingham bus from Braintree stops at the Railway (except on Sundays)
Car Parking: Parking at the site
Coach Parking: Free parking at site
Souvenir Shop(s): Yes
Food & Drinks: Yes – on operational days. Also Pullman Sunday Lunches – bookings necessary.

SPECIAL INFORMATION

The railway is being re-built on a section of the old Colne Valley & Halstead Railway, with all buildings, bridges, signal boxes, etc. re-located on site.
The Railway also has a Farm Park to visit on site (open between 1st May and 24th September only).

OPERATING INFORMATION

Opening Times: Trains run every Sunday and Bank Holiday weekend from 4th March to 28th October. Open daily in August except for Mondays and Fridays. Pre-booked parties any time by arrangement and various other special events.
Steam Working: Sundays 12.00pm to 4.00pm, Bank Holidays from 11.00am to 4.00pm and 11.30am to 3.30pm on midweek operating days.
Prices: Adult – Steam days £6.00; Diesel £5.00
　　　　　Child – Steam £4.00; Diesel £3.00
　　　　　Family (2 adults + 4 children) –
　　　　　　　　Steam £20.00; Diesel £16.00
　　　　　Senior Citizen – Steam £5.00; Diesel £4.00

Detailed Directions by Car:
The Railway is situated on the A1017 between Halstead and Haverhill, 7 miles north-west of Braintree.

CRICH TRAMWAY VILLAGE

Address: Crich Tramway Village, Crich, Matlock, Derbyshire DE4 5DP	**No of Steam Locos:** None
Telephone No: (01773) 854321	**No of Other Locos:** 50 trams approx.
Year Formed: 1964	**No of Members:** 2,500
Location of Line: Crich	**Annual Membership Fee:** £20.00
Length of Line: 1 mile	**Approx No of Visitors P.A.:** 100,000
	Web site: www.tramway.co.uk

GENERAL INFORMATION

Nearest Mainline Station: Whatstandwell (1 mile)
Nearest Bus Station: Crich
Car Parking: Free parking available on site
Coach Parking: Free parking available on site
Souvenir Shop(s): Yes
Food & Drinks: Yes

SPECIAL INFORMATION

The admission price includes unlimited tram rides plus a host of indoor attractions.

OPERATING INFORMATION

Opening Times: 10.30am to 4.00pm daily from 10th to 25th February and in weekends in March. Open daily from 31st March to 28th October 10.00am to 5.30pm then weekends in November and December (until 16th) from 10.30am to 4.00pm.
Steam Working: On certain Special event days only – please phone for details.
Prices: Adult £9.50 (£10.50 for Premier events)
  Child £5.00 (£5.50 for Premier events)
  Senior Citizen £8.50 (£9.50 Premier)
  Family Tickets £26.00 (£28.50 Premier)

Detailed Directions by Car:
From All Parts: The Museum is situated just of the B5035 near Crich – this is approximately 15 miles north of Derby. Exit the M1 at Junction 28 if travelling from the North or Junction 26 from the South.

DARLINGTON RAILWAY CENTRE & MUSEUM

Address: North Road Station, Darlington, Co. Durham   DL3 6ST
Telephone Nº: (01325) 460532
Year Formed: 1975
Location of Line: Adjacent to North Road Station
Length of Line: ¼ mile

Nº of Steam Locos: 5
Nº of Other Locos: –
Nº of Members: –
Annual Membership Fee: –
Approx Nº of Visitors P.A.: 27,091
Gauge: Standard
Web site: www.drcm.org.uk

GENERAL INFORMATION

Nearest Mainline Station: North Road (adjacent)
Nearest Bus Station: Darlington (1 mile)
Car Parking: Free parking at site
Coach Parking: Free parking at site
Souvenir Shop(s): Yes
Food & Drinks: Cafe open 11.00am to 3.00pm. Drinks machine and confectionery at other times.

SPECIAL INFORMATION

The museum is an 1842 station on the route of the Stockton and Darlington Railway and is devoted to the Railways of north-east England.

OPERATING INFORMATION

Opening Times: The Museum is open 10.00am to 5.00pm daily except Christmas Day, Boxing Day and New Year's Day.
The Locomotive Works run by the A1 Steam Locomotive Trust is usually open on the 2nd Saturday of each month.
Steam Working: At various Special events throughout the year – please phone for details.
Prices: Adult £2.50
Child £1.50
Senior Citizen £1.50
Family Ticket £7.50

Detailed Directions by Car:
From Darlington Town Centre: Follow the A167 north for about ¾ mile then turn left immediately before the Railway bridge; From A1(M): Exit at Junction 59 then follow A167 towards Darlington and turn right after passing under the Railway bridge.

THE DARTMOOR RAILWAY

Address: Okehampton Station, Station Road, Okehampton   EX20 1EH
Telephone Nº: (01837) 55637
Year Formed: 1997
Location of Line: Meldon Quarry to Coleford Junction

Length of Line: 15 miles
Nº of Steam Locos: 1
Nº of Other Locos: 3 and DMUs
Gauge: Standard
Web site: www.dartmoorrailway.co.uk

GENERAL INFORMATION

Nearest Mainline Station: Crediton
Nearest Bus Station: Okehampton
Car Parking: Okehampton Station and some spaces at Sampford Courtenay Station – all free of charge
Coach Parking: Okehampton Station
Souvenir Shop(s): Yes
Food & Drinks: Okehampton Buffet is open daily from 8.30am. Melton Buffet is open weekends and Bank Holidays throughout the year and during the summer holidays. Both Buffets are fully licensed.

SPECIAL INFORMATION

2007 is the 10th anniversary of the re-opening of Okehampton Station following restoration. The railway operates on the route of the old Southern Railway line through the mid-Devon countryside to the northern slopes of Dartmoor National Park. Cycle hire is available at Okehampton Station

OPERATING INFORMATION

Opening Times: Okehampton Station is open daily. A regular Meldon to Okehampton service runs at weekends all year round, Bank Holidays and summer holidays. Weekday services are subject to change. Contact the railway for further details.
Steam Working: Generally on Sundays and some weekdays during the summer plus special events.
Prices: Prices vary depending on the service.

Detailed Directions by Car:
From All Parts: Take the A30 Exeter to Launceston dual carriageway and exit at the Okehampton turn-off. Once in town, follow the brown tourist signs up the hill to Okehampton Station.

DEAN FOREST RAILWAY

Address: Norchard Centre, Forest Road; Lydney, Gloucestershire GL15 4ET
Telephone Nº: (01594) 845840
Information Line: (01594) 843423 (24 hr.)
Year Formed: 1970
Location of Line: Lydney, Gloucestershire
Length of Line: 4½ miles

Nº of Steam Locos: 7 (2 working)
Nº of Other Locos: 18
Nº of Members: 1,000
Annual Membership Fee: Adult £14.00; Family (4 persons) £17.00
Approx Nº of Visitors P.A.: 55,000
Gauge: Standard
Web site: www.deanforestrailway.co.uk

GENERAL INFORMATION

Nearest Mainline Station: Lydney (200 metres)
Nearest Bus Station: Lydney (1 mile)
Car Parking: 600 spaces available at Norchard
Coach Parking: Ample space available
Souvenir Shop(s): Yes + a Museum
Food & Drinks: Yes – on operational days only

SPECIAL INFORMATION

Dean Forest Railway preserves the sole surviving line of the Severn and Wye Railway. The Railway has lengthened the line to a total of 4½ miles and Norchard to Parkend is now open for steam train operation giving a round trip of 9 miles.

OPERATING INFORMATION

Opening Times: Norchard is open every day for viewing. Trains operate on Sundays from the end of March to the end of October. Also on Wednesdays and Saturdays from June to September and on various other dates. Please phone or check the railway's web site for further details as required.
Steam Working: Most services are steam-hauled – phone for details. Trains depart Norchard at various times from 10.55am to 3.30pm.
Prices: Adult Return £9.00
    Child Return £5.00 (ages 5-16 years old)
    Senior Citizens £8.00
N.B. Fares may differ on special dates.

Detailed Directions by Car:
From M50 & Ross-on-Wye: Take the B4228 and B4234 via Coleford to reach Lydney. Norchard is located on the B4234, ¾ mile north of Lydney Town Centre; From Monmouth: Take the A4136 and B4431 onto the B4234 via Coleford; From South Wales: Take the M4 then M48 onto the A48 via Chepstow to Lydney; From Midlands/Gloucester: Take the M5 to Gloucester then the A48 to Lydney; From the West Country: Take the M4 and M48 via the 'Old' Severn Bridge to Chepstow and then the A48 to Lydney.

DERWENT VALLEY LIGHT RAILWAY

Address: Murton Park, Murton Lane, Murton, York YO19 5UF	**N° of Steam Locos:** 2
	N° of Other Locos: 5
Telephone N°: (01904) 489966	**N° of Members:** 80
Year Formed: 1991	**Annual Membership Fee:** £10.00
Location of Line: Murton, near York	**Approx N° of Visitors P.A.:** 15,000
Length of Line: ½ mile	**Gauge:** Standard
	Web site: www.dvlr.org.uk

GENERAL INFORMATION

Nearest Mainline Station: York (4 miles)
Nearest Bus Station: York (4 miles)
Car Parking: Large free car park at the site
Coach Parking: Free at the site
Souvenir Shop(s): Yes
Food & Drinks: Yes – as above

SPECIAL INFORMATION

The site is the remnants of the Derwent Valley
Railway which was the last privately owned railway
in England, originally opened in 1913.

OPERATING INFORMATION

Opening Times: Sundays and Bank Holidays from
Easter until the end of September. Also Santa
Specials run in December.
Steam Working: Second and last Sunday in the
month and Bank Holidays – 10.30am to 4.30pm.
Prices: Adult £5.00
Child £3.00
Senior Citizens/Students £4.00
Family Tickets £12.00 (2 adult + 4 child)
Prices are for entrance to the Yorkshire Museum of
Farming – train rides are included in the price.

Detailed Directions by Car:
From All Parts: The railway is well signposted for the Yorkshire Museum of Farming from the A64 (York to
Scarborough road), the A1079 (York to Hull road) and the A166 (York to Bridlington road).

DIDCOT RAILWAY CENTRE

Address: Didcot Railway Centre, Didcot, Oxfordshire OX11 7NJ
Telephone Nº: (01235) 817200
Year Formed: 1961
Location of Line: Didcot
Length of Line: ¾ mile
Gauge: Standard and 7 foot ¼ inch

Nº of Steam Locos: 23
Nº of Other Locos: 2
Nº of Members: 4,400
Annual Membership Fee: Full £26.00; Over 60/Under 18 £18.00; Family £33.00
Approx Nº of Visitors P.A.: 70,000
Web Site: www.didcotrailwaycentre.org.uk

GENERAL INFO

Nearest Mainline Station: Didcot Parkway (adjacent)
Nearest Bus Station: Buses to Didcot call at the Railway station
Car Parking: BR car park adjacent
Coach Parking: Further details on application
Souvenir Shop(s): Yes
Food & Drinks: Yes

SPECIAL INFO

The Centre is based on a Great Western Railway engine shed and is devoted to the re-creation of part of the GWR including Brunel's broad gauge railway and a newly built replica of the Fire Fly locomotive of 1840.

OPERATING INFO

Opening Times: Weekends all year round, open daily during most school holidays and then from 23rd June to 2nd September. Weekends and Steam days open 10.00am to 5.00pm. Other days and during Winter open 10.00am to 4.00pm.
Steam Working: All Weekends and Bank Holidays from 28th April to 2nd September. Wednesdays from 4th July to 29th August. Phone for details of Autumn steam days or alternatively check the web site.
Prices: Adult £4.00–£9.50
Child £3.00–£7.50
Discounted family tickets are often available (2 adults + 2 children). Prices vary depending on the events.

Detailed Directions by Car:
From East & West: Take the M4 to Junction 13 then the A34 and A4130 (follow brown Tourist signs to Didcot Railway Centre); From North: The Centre is signed from the A34 to A4130.

DOWNPATRICK & COUNTY DOWN RAILWAY

Address: Market Street, Downpatrick, Co. Down, Northern Ireland	**Nº of Steam Locos:** 3
Telephone Nº: (07790) 802049	**Nº of Other Locos:** 5
Year Formed: 1985	**Nº of Members:** 180
Location of Line: Downpatrick	**Annual Membership Fee:** Adult £20.00, Family £25.00, Concessions £15.00
Length of Line: 2 miles	**Approx Nº of Visitors P.A.:** 13,000
Gauge: Irish Standard (5 foot 3 inches)	**Web:** www.downrail.co.uk

GENERAL INFORMATION

Nearest Mainline Station: –
Nearest Bus Station: Adjacent to Station
Car Parking: Ample parking adjacent to Station
Coach Parking: Ample parking adjacent to Station
Souvenir Shop(s): Yes
Food & Drinks: Yes

SPECIAL INFORMATION

This is the only operating Standard (5' 3") Gauge Heritage Railway in Ireland.

OPERATING INFORMATION

Opening Times: The Museum is open daily from June to September.
Steam Working: Weekends from 16th June to 9th September (includes August Bank Holiday). Trains are usually steam hauled and run from 1.40pm to 5.00pm. Special trains run at Easter, Halloween and Christmas.
Prices: Adult Return £4.50 (Single £3.00)
Child Return £3.50 (Single £2.50)

Detailed Directions by Car:
From Belfast take the A7 Downpatrick Road. Upon arrival in Downpatrick, follow the brown tourist signs and the Railway Museum is adjacent to the bus station.

EAST ANGLIAN RAILWAY MUSEUM

Address: Chappel & Wakes Colne
Station, Colchester, Essex   CO6 2DS
Telephone Nº: (01206) 242524
Year Formed: 1969
Location of Line: 6 miles west of
Colchester on Marks Tey to Sudbury branch
Length of Line: A third of a mile

Nº of Steam Locos: 8   **Other Locos:** 4
Nº of Members: 750
Annual Membership Fee: Adult £20.00;
Senior Citizen £15.00
Approx Nº of Visitors P.A.: 40,000
Gauge: Standard
Web site: www.earm.co.uk

GENERAL INFORMATION

Nearest Mainline Station: Chappel & Wakes Colne
(adajcent)
Nearest Bus Stop: Chappel (400 yards)
Car Parking: Free parking at site
Coach Parking: Free parking at site
Souvenir Shop(s): Yes
Food & Drinks: Yes – drinks are available every day
and snacks are also available on operating days.

SPECIAL INFORMATION

The museum has the most comprehensive collection
of railway architecture & engineering in the region.
The railway also has a miniature railway that usually
operates on steam days.

OPERATING INFORMATION

Opening Times: Open daily 10.00am to 5.00pm.
Steam days open from 11.00am to 5.00pm
Steam Working: Steam days are held every month
from April to August and also in October and
December. Bank Holidays are also Steam days.
Check the web site for further details.
Prices: Adult   £3.00 non-Steam; £6.00 Steam
          Child   £2.00 non-Steam; £3.00 Steam
          O.A.P.   £2.50 non-Steam; £4.50 Steam
          Family   £8.00 non-Steam; £15.00 Steam
Children under the age of 4 are admitted free of
charge. A 10% discount is available for bookings for
more than 10 people.

Detailed Directions by Car:
From North & South: Turn off the A12 south west of Colchester onto the A1124 (formerly the A604). The
Museum is situated just off the A1124; From West: Turn off the A120 just before Marks Tey (signposted).

EAST KENT RAILWAY

Address: Station Road, Shepherdswell, Dover, Kent CT15 7PD	**N° of Steam Locos:** 1
Telephone N°: (01304) 832042	**N° of Other Locos:** 7 + 2 DMUs
Year Formed: 1985	**N° of Members:** 400
Location of Line: Between Shepherdswell and Eythorne	**Annual Membership Fee:** £15.00 (Adult)
	Approx N° of Visitors P.A.: 4,500
Length of Line: 2 miles	**Gauge:** Standard and also 5 inch and 3¼ inch miniature gauges
	Web site: www.eastkentrailway.co.uk

GENERAL INFORMATION

Nearest Mainline Station: Shepherdswell (50 yards)
Car Parking: Available Shepherdswell and Eythorne
Coach Parking: In adjacent Station Yard
Souvenir Shop(s): Yes
Food & Drinks: Yes

SPECIAL INFORMATION

The East Kent Railway was originally built between 1911 and 1917 to service Tilmanstone Colliery. Closed in the mid-1980's, the railway was re-opened in 1995.

OPERATING INFORMATION

Opening Times: Open weekends throughout the year for static viewing from 11.00am to 3.00pm. Trains run during Easter and Sundays from May to September and also weekends in December.
Steam Working: None at present.
Prices: Adult £6.00
         Child £3.00
         Senior Citizens £5.00

Detailed Directions by Car:
From the A2: Take the turning to Shepherdswell and continue to the village. Pass the shop on the left and cross the railway bridge. Take the next left (Station Road) signposted at the traffic lights for the EKR; From the A256: Take the turning for Eythorne at the roundabout on the section between Eastry and Whitfield. Follow the road through Eythorne. Further on you will cross the railway line and enter Shepherdswell. After a few hundred yards take the right turn signposted for the EKR.

EAST LANCASHIRE RAILWAY

Address: Bolton Street Station, Bury, Lancashire BL9 0EY	**Nº of Steam Locos:** 14
Telephone Nº: (0161) 764-7790	**Nº of Other Locos:** 16
Year Formed: 1968	**Nº of Members:** 4,500
Location of Line: Heywood, Bury and Rawtenstall	**Annual Membership Fee:** £17.00
	Approx Nº of Visitors P.A.: 110,000
	Gauge: Standard
Length of Line: 12 miles	**Web site:** www.east-lancs-rly.co.uk

GENERAL INFORMATION

Nearest Mainline Station: Manchester (then Metro Link to Bury)
Nearest Bus Station: ¼ mile
Car Parking: Adjacent
Coach Parking: Adjacent
Souvenir Shop(s): Yes
Food & Drinks: Yes

SPECIAL INFORMATION

Originally opened in 1846, the East Lancashire Railway was re-opened in 1991.

OPERATING INFORMATION

Opening Times: Every weekend & Bank Holiday 9.00am to 5.00pm. Also Wednesday to Friday from May to September inclusive. A number of special events also run throughout the year.
Steam Working: Most trains are steam-hauled. Saturdays alternate Steam & Diesel. 2 engines in steam on Sundays.
Prices: Adult Return £11.00
  Child Return £7.40
  Family Return £29.40
Cheaper fares are available for shorter journeys.

Detailed Directions by Car:
From All Parts: Exit the M66 at Junction 2 and take the A56 into Bury. Follow the brown tourist signs and turn right into Bolton Street at the junction with the A58. The station is about 150 yards on the right.

EAST SOMERSET RAILWAY (STRAWBERRY LINE)

Address: Cranmore Railway Station, Shepton Mallet, Somerset BA4 4QP
Telephone Nº: (01749) 880417
Year Formed: 1971
Location of Line: Cranmore, off A361 between Frome and Shepton Mallet
Length of Line: 3 miles

Nº of Steam Locos: 5
Nº of Other Locos: 2
Nº of Members: 480
Annual Membership Fee: Single £15.00; Couple £19.00; Family £28.00
Approx Nº of Visitors P.A.: 20,000
Gauge: Standard

GENERAL INFORMATION

Nearest Mainline Station: Castle Cary (10 miles)
Nearest Bus Station: Shepton Mallet (3 miles)
Car Parking: Space for 100 cars available
Coach Parking: Available by arrangement
Souvenir Shop(s): Yes
Food & Drinks: Yes

SPECIAL INFORMATION

Footplate experience courses available – phone (01749) 880417 for further details.

Web site: www.eastsomersetrailway.com

OPERATING INFORMATION

Opening Times: Complex, Museum and Engine Sheds open daily except for 25th and 26th December and throughout January and February.
Steam Working: Sundays in the Winter, weekends and bank holidays in April, May & October plus some weekdays in the Summer. Santa Specials run on weekends in December. Other special events run on various dates. Open 10.00am to 4.00pm in the Winter, 10.00am to 5.30pm in the Summer.
Prices: Adults £6.50   Children £4.50
Senior Citizens £5.50
Family £19.00

Detailed Directions by Car:
From the North: Take A367/A37 to Shepton Mallet then turn left onto A361 to Frome. Carry on to Shepton Mallet and 9 miles after Frome turn left at Cranmore; From the South: Take A36 to Frome bypass then A361 to Cranmore; From the West: Take A371 from Wells to Shepton Mallet, then A361 to Frome (then as above).

ECCLESBOURNE VALLEY RAILWAY

Address: Station Road, Coldwell Street, Wirksworth   DE4 4FB
Telephone Nº: (01629) 823076
Year Formed: 2000
Location of Line: Wirksworth to Duffield
Length of Line: 1½ miles

Nº of Steam Locos: 3
Nº of Other Locos: 9
Nº of Members: 600+
Annual Membership Fee: £12.00
Approx Nº of Visitors P.A.: 15,000
Gauge: Standard
Web site: www.evra.org.uk

GENERAL INFORMATION

Nearest Mainline Station: Cromford (2 miles)
Nearest Bus Station: Derby (13 miles)
Car Parking: Available at the Station
Coach Parking: Available at the Station
Souvenir Shop(s): Yes
Food & Drinks: Yes

SPECIAL INFORMATION

The line is being restored section by section with a view to completing all 8½ miles by 2008.

OPERATING INFORMATION

Opening Times: Open for viewing most days from 10.00am to 4.00pm. Trains running in 2007: 6th-9th April; 5th-7th and 26th-28th May; 23rd & 24th June; 15th July; 25th-27th August; 8th, 9th, 15th & 16th September. Also Santa Specials on 15th, 16th, 22nd and 23rd December.
Steam Working: None at present.
Prices: Adult Tickets £5.00 (travel all day)
          Child Tickets £2.50 (travel all day)
          Concessions Tickets £3.50 (travel all day)
Note: Prices may be higher for some special events.

Detailed Directions by Car:
From All Parts: Exit the M1 at Junction 26 and take the A610 Ambergate then the A6 to Whatstandwell. Turn left onto the B5035 to Wirksworth and the station is at the bottom of the hill as you enter the town.

ELSECAR RAILWAY

Address: Wath Road, Elsecar, Barnsley, S74 8HJ
Telephone Nº: (01226) 746746
Year Formed: 2002
Location of Line: Elsecar, near Barnsley
Length of Line: 1 mile

Nº of Steam Locos: 2
Nº of Other Locos: 4
Nº of Members: Approximately 64
Annual Membership Fee: £10.00
Approx Nº of Visitors P.A.: 20,000
Gauge: Standard
Web site: www.elsecarrailway.cjb.net

GENERAL INFORMATION

Nearest Mainline Station: Elsecar
Nearest Bus Station: Barnsley
Car Parking: Large free car park at the site
Coach Parking: At the site
Souvenir Shop(s): Yes
Food & Drinks: Yes

SPECIAL INFORMATION

The Railway is based at the Elsecar Heritage Centre which is an antiques and craft centre with a wide range of displays and special events.

OPERATING INFORMATION

Opening Times: The Heritage Centre is open daily from 10.00am to 5.00pm throughout the year except from 25th December to 2nd January.
Steam Working: Trains run on Sundays from March to October – hourly from 12.00pm to 4.00pm and on special event days. Steam may be replaced by diesel when required. Please phone for details.
Prices: Adults £3.00
Children £1.50
Senior Citizens £2.00
Admission to the museum and site is free of charge except for during Special Events.

Detailed Directions by Car:
From All Parts: Exit the M1 at Junction 36 and follow the brown 'Elsecar Heritage' signs taking the A6135 for approximately 2 miles. Turn left onto Broad Carr Road for just under a mile, then right onto Armroyd Lane and right again onto Fitzwilliam Street. Free visitor car parking is available on Wentworth Road off the junction of Fitzwilliam Street and Wath Road.

EMBSAY & BOLTON ABBEY STEAM RAILWAY

Address: Bolton Abbey Station, Bolton Abbey, Skipton, N. Yorkshire BD23 6AF	**Nº of Steam Locos**: 20
Telephone Nº: (01756) 710614	**Nº of Other Locos**: 12
Year Formed: 1968	**Nº of Members**: 700
Location of Line: 2 miles east of Skipton	**Annual Membership Fee**: £10.00
Length of Line: 4½ miles	**Approx Nº of Visitors P.A.**: 107,000
	Gauge: Standard

GENERAL INFORMATION

Nearest Mainline Station: Skipton (2 miles), Ilkley (3 miles)
Nearest Bus Station: Skipton (2 miles), Ilkley (3 mls)
Car Parking: Large car park at both Stations
Coach Parking: Large coach park at both Stations
Souvenir Shop(s): Yes
Food & Drinks: Yes – Cafe + Buffet cars

SPECIAL INFORMATION

The line extension to Bolton Abbey opened in 1998.

Web site: www.embsayboltonabbeyrailway.org.uk

OPERATING INFORMATION

Opening Times: Every Sunday throughout the year. Weekends from Easter to the end of October and daily in the summer season and October half-term. Tuesdays in June and September. Santa Specials run on December weekends.
Steam Working: Steam trains depart Embsay Station at 10.30am, 12.00pm, 1.30pm, 3.00pm and 4.30pm on most days during the Main Season though certain days are operated by a heritage D.M.U. Contact the railway for further details.
Prices: Adult Return £7.00
Child Return £3.50
Family Ticket £18.00 (2 adult + 2 children)
Different fares may apply on special event days.

Detailed Directions by Car:
From All Parts: Embsay Station is off the A59 Skipton bypass by the Harrogate Road. Bolton Abbey Station is off the A59 at Bolton Abbey.

EPPING ONGAR RAILWAY

Address: Ongar Station, Ongar, Essex, CM5 9BN
Telephone Nº: (01277) 366616
Year Formed: 2004
Location of Line: Epping to Ongar
Length of Line: 6 miles

Nº of Steam Locos: 5 (One in steam)
Nº of Other Locos: 4
Nº of Members: None
Annual Membership Fee: –
Approx Nº of Visitors P.A.: 60,000
Gauge: Standard gauge and also 5 feet
Web site: www.eorailway.co.uk

GENERAL INFORMATION

Nearest Mainline Station: Epping L.U.L. (6½ miles from Ongar Station)
Nearest Bus Station: Epping (6½ miles)
Car Parking: Limited free parking at Ongar and North Weald stations. Parking is available at the London Underground station in Epping.
Coach Parking: By arrangement only
Souvenir Shop(s): Yes
Food & Drinks: Available

SPECIAL INFORMATION

The Railway has 5 Finnish locomotives on display which unfortunately are not able to use the line due to their 5 foot gauge.

OPERATING INFORMATION

Opening Times: Sundays only throughout the year. 11.00am to 3.00pm during the Winter then open until 4.00pm during the Summer.
Steam Working: None at present
Prices: Adult £5.00
  Child £3.00 (Under-5s travel free)
  Concessions £3.00
  Family £12.00 (2 adults + 3 children)

Detailed Directions by Car:
For North Weald Station: Exit the M11 at Junction 7 and follow the A414 towards Chelmsford and North Weald. Take the 3rd exit at the 2nd roundabout ('The Talbot' pub on the left) and follow the road into North Weald village. Station Road is on the left just after leaving the village. For Ongar Station: Exit the M11 at Junction 7 and follow the A414 towards Chelmsford and North Weald. Follow the road for approximately 5 miles going straight on at two roundabouts. At the 3rd roundabout (BP garage on the left) take the third exit towards Ongar. Epping Ongar Railway is located approximately on the right hand side after approximately 400 yards.
At present there is no connection at the Epping end of the line but parking is available at the London Underground Station in Epping and a vintage bus connects with the line at North Weald.

FOXFIELD STEAM RAILWAY

Address: Caverswall Road Station, Blythe Bridge, Stoke-on-Trent, Staffs. ST11 9EA	**Nº of Steam Locos**: 16
Telephone Nº: (01782) 396210	**Nº of Other Locos**: 15
Year Formed: 1967	**Nº of Members**: Over 300
Location of Line: Blythe Bridge	**Annual Membership Fee**: Adult £12.00; Junior £6.00; Family £20.00
Length of Line: 3½ miles	**Approx Nº of Visitors P.A.**: 25,000
Gauge: Standard	**Web site**: www.foxfieldrailway.co.uk

GENERAL INFORMATION

Nearest Mainline Station: Blythe Bridge (¼ mile)
Nearest Bus Station: Hanley (5 miles)
Car Parking: Space for 300 cars available
Coach Parking: Space for 6 coaches available
Souvenir Shop(s): Yes
Food & Drinks: Yes – Buffet and Real Ale Bar

SPECIAL INFORMATION

The Railway is a former Colliery railway built in 1893 to take coal from Foxfield Colliery. It has the steepest Standard Gauge adhesion worked gradient in the UK and freight trains can be seen on these gradients during the annual Steam Gala in July.

OPERATING INFORMATION

Opening Times: Sundays & Bank Holiday Mondays from Easter to the end of October. Also weekends in December. Open 10.30am to 5.00pm.
Steam Working: 11.30am, 1.00pm, 2.00pm, 3.00pm & 4.00pm although Special Event days run earlier also.
Prices: Adult Tickets – £7.50
Child Tickets £1.00 (3-16 years old)
Senior Citizen Tickets – £6.50
Fares may vary on special event days.

Detailed Directions by Car:
From South: Exit M6 at Junction 14 onto the A34 to Stone then the A520 to Meir and the A50 to Blythe Bridge; From North: Exit M6 at Junction 15 then the A500 to Stoke-on-Trent and the A50 to Blythe Bridge; From East: Take the A50 to Blythe Bridge. Once in Blythe Bridge, turn by the Mainline crossing.

GLOUCESTERSHIRE WARWICKSHIRE RAILWAY

Address: The Station, Toddington, Cheltenham, Gloucestershire GL54 5DT
Telephone Nº: (01242) 621405
Year Formed: 1981
Location of Line: 5 miles south of Broadway, Worcestershire, near the A46
Length of Line: 10 miles

Nº of Steam Locos: 11
Nº of Other Locos: 17
Nº of Members: 2,650
Annual Membership Fee: £14.00 (Adult)
Approx Nº of Visitors P.A.: 50,000
Gauge: Standard and Narrow gauge
Web site: www.gwsr.com

GENERAL INFORMATION

Nearest Mainline Station: Cheltenham Spa or Ashchurch
Nearest Bus Station: Cheltenham
Car Parking: Parking available at Toddington, Winchcombe & Cheltenham Racecourse Stations
Coach Parking: Parking available as above
Souvenir Shop(s): Yes
Food & Drinks: Yes

SPECIAL INFORMATION

The North Gloucestershire narrow gauge railway also runs from Toddington Station. Gotherington Halt is now open with access by foot only.

OPERATING INFORMATION

Opening Times: Weekends and Bank Holidays from March to December. Also daily during School Holidays. 10.00am to 5.00pm
Steam Working: Most operating days
Prices: Adult Return £10.00
　　　　Child Return £6.00
　　　　Senior Citizen Return £8.50
　　　　Family Return £27.00 (2 Adult + 3 Child)
　　　　Under 5's travel free of charge

Detailed Directions by Car:
Toddington is 11 miles north east of Cheltenham, 5 miles south of Broadway just off the B4632 (old A46). Exit the M5 at Junction 9 towards Stow-on-the-Wold for the B4632. The Railway is clearly visible from the B4632.

GREAT CENTRAL RAILWAY

Address: Great Central Station, Great Central Road, Loughborough, Leicestershire LE11 1RW **Telephone Nº:** (01509) 230726 **Year Formed:** 1969 **Location of Line:** From Loughborough to Leicester	**Length of Line:** 8 miles **Nº of Steam Locos:** 10 **Nº of Other Locos:** 11 **Nº of Members:** 5,000 **Annual Membership Fee:** £25.00 **Approx Nº of Visitors P.A.:** 150,000 **Gauge:** Standard

GENERAL INFORMATION

Nearest Mainline Station: Loughborough (1 mile)
Nearest Bus Station: Loughborough (½ mile)
Car Parking: Street parking outside the Station
Coach Parking: Car parks at Quorn & Woodhouse, Rothley and Leicester North
Souvenir Shop(s): Yes
Food & Drinks: Yes – Buffet or Restaurant cars are usually available for snacks or other meals

Web site: www.gcrailway.co.uk

SPECIAL INFORMATION

The aim of the GCR is to recreate the experience of British main line railway operation during the best years of steam locomotives.

OPERATING INFORMATION

Opening Times: Open daily throughout the year.
Steam Working: Weekends, Bank Holidays and some Special Events throughout the year. Also selected weekdays from May to September.
Prices: Adult Day ticket £12.00
Child/Senior Citizen Day ticket £8.00
Family Day Ticket £30 (2 adults + 3 children)

Detailed Directions by Car:
Great Central Road is on the South East side of Loughborough and is clearly signposted from the A6 Leicester Road and A60 Nottingham Road.

GWILI RAILWAY

Address: Bronwydd Arms Station,
Bronwydd Arms, Carmarthen SA33 6HT
Telephone N°: (01267) 230666
Year Formed: 1975
Location of Line: Near Carmarthen,
South Wales
Length of Line: 2½ miles

N° of Steam Locos: 5
N° of Other Locos: 6
N° of Members: 900 shareholders,
450 Society members
Annual Membership Fee: £10.00
Approx N° of Visitors P.A.: 24,000
Gauge: Standard
Web site: www.gwili-railway.co.uk

GENERAL INFORMATION

Nearest Mainline Station: Carmarthen (3 miles)
Nearest Bus Station: Carmarthen (3 miles)
Car Parking: Free parking at Bronwydd Arms
except for a few special occasions
Coach Parking: Free parking at Bronwydd Arms
(but by arrangement only)
Souvenir Shop(s): Yes
Food & Drinks: Yes

SPECIAL INFORMATION

Gwili Railway was the first Standard Gauge
preserved railway in Wales. There is a riverside
picnic area and Miniature railway at Llwyfan Cerrig
Station.

OPERATING INFORMATION

Opening Times: Wednesdays and Sundays in June
and July. Daily in August except for Saturdays and
most Mondays/Tuesdays. Open Sundays in
September and most weekends in December for
Santa Specials. Please phone for further details.
Steam Working: Most advertised trains are steam
hauled. Trains run from 11.15am to 4.30pm in high
season and until 3.45pm at some other times.
Prices: Adult £5.50
    Child £3.00
    Family £15.00 (2 adults + up to 2 children)
    Senior Citizens £4.50
Note: Discounts available for groups of 10 or more.

Detailed Directions by Car:
The Railway is three miles North of Carmarthen – signposted off the A484 Carmarthen to Cardigan Road.

HOLLYCOMBE STEAM COLLECTION

Address: Hollycombe, Liphook, Hants. GU30 7LP
Telephone Nº: (01428) 724900
Year Formed: 1970
Location of Line: Hollycombe, Liphook
Length of Line: 1¾ miles Narrow gauge, ¼ mile Standard gauge

Nº of Steam Locos: 3
Nº of Other Locos: 1
Nº of Members: 100
Annual Membership Fee: £8.00
Approx Nº of Visitors P.A.: 35,000
Gauge: 2 feet plus Standard & 7¼ inches
Web site: www.hollycombe.co.uk

GENERAL INFORMATION

Nearest Mainline Station: Liphook (1 mile)
Nearest Bus Station: Liphook
Car Parking: Extensive grass area
Coach Parking: Hardstanding
Souvenir Shop(s): Yes
Food & Drinks: Yes – Cafe

SPECIAL INFORMATION

The narrow gauge railway ascends to spectacular views of the Downs and is part of an extensive working steam museum.

OPERATING INFORMATION

Opening Times: Sundays and Bank Holidays from 1st April to 7th October. Open daily from 29th July to 27th August.
Steam Working: 1.00pm to 5.00pm
Prices: Adult £10.00
Child £8.50
Senior Citizen £9.00
Family £35.00 (2 adults + 3 children)
Note: Prices are £1.00 less on Summer weekdays

Detailed Directions by Car:
Take the A3 to Liphook and follow the brown tourist signs for the railway.

ISLE OF WIGHT STEAM RAILWAY

Address: The Railway Station, Haven Street, Ryde, Isle of Wight PO33 4DS
Telephone Nº: (01983) 882204
Year Formed: 1971 (re-opened)
Location: Smallbrook Junction to Wootton
Length of Line: 5 miles
Nº of Steam Locos: 7

Nº of Other Locos: 3
Nº of Members: 1,300
Annual Membership Fee: £15.00
Approx Nº of Visitors P.A.: 100,000
Gauge: Standard
Talking Timetable: (01983) 884343
Web site: www.iwsteamrailway.co.uk

GENERAL INFORMATION

Nearest Mainline Station: Smallbrook Junction (direct interchange)
Nearest Bus: From Ryde & Newport direct
Car Parking: Free parking at Havenstreet & Wootton Stations
Coach Parking: Free at Havenstreet Station
Souvenir Shop(s): Yes – at Havenstreet Station
Food & Drinks: Yes – at Havenstreet Station

SPECIAL INFORMATION

The IWSR uses mostly Victorian & Edwardian locomotives and carriages to recreate the atmosphere of an Isle of Wight branch line railway.

OPERATING INFORMATION

Opening Times: Selected days between March and October and daily from late May to mid-September
Steam Working: 10.30am to 4.00pm (depending on the Station)
Prices: Adult Return £8.50
Child Return £4.50
Family Return £22.00
(2 adults + 2 children)

Detailed Directions by Car:
To reach the Isle of Wight head for the Ferry ports at Lymington, Southampton or Portsmouth. From all parts of the Isle of Wight, head for Ryde and follow the brown tourist signs.

KEIGHLEY & WORTH VALLEY RAILWAY

Address: The Station, Haworth, Keighley, West Yorkshire BD22 8NJ
Telephone Nº: (01535) 645214 (enquiries); (01535) 647777 (24 hour timetable)
Year Formed: 1962 (Line re-opened 1968)
Location of Line: From Keighley southwards through Haworth to Oxenhope
Length of Line: 4¾ miles

Nº of Steam Locos: 30
Nº of Other Locos: 10
Members: 4,500 (350 working members)
Annual Membership Fee: Adult £17.00; Adult life membership £340.00
Approx Nº of Visitors P.A.: 150,000
Gauge: Standard
Web Site: www.kwvr.co.uk

GENERAL INFORMATION

Nearest Mainline Station: Keighley (adjacent)
Nearest Bus Station: Keighley (5 minutes walk)
Car Parking: Parking at Keighley, Ingrow, Haworth (charged) and Oxenhope
Coach Parking: At Ingrow & Oxenhope (phone in advance)
Souvenir Shop(s): Yes – at Keighley, Haworth & Oxenhope
Food & Drinks: Yes – at Keighley & Oxenhope when trains run.

OPERATING INFORMATION

Opening Times: Weekends & Bank Holidays throughout the year. Daily from 1st July to 2nd September. Also open during Easter, Whit, October School holidays and 26th December to 1st January.
Steam Working: Early trains are Diesel; Steam runs from mid-morning on all operating days (except 4 weekends prior to Christmas).
Prices: Adult Return £9.00; £12.00 day rover
Child Return £4.50; £6.00 day rover
Family Return £22.00 (2 adults, 3 children)
Family Day Rover £27.00

Detailed Directions by Car:
Exit the M62 at Junction 26 and take the M606 to its' end. Follow the ring-road signs around Bradford to Shipley. Take the A650 through Bingley to Keighley and follow the brown tourist signs to the railway. Alternatively, take the A6033 from Hebden Bridge to Oxenhope and follow the brown signs to Oxenhope or Haworth Stations.

KENT & EAST SUSSEX RAILWAY

Address: Tenterden Town Station, Tenterden, Kent   TN30 6HE
Telephone Nº: 087 060 060 74
Year Formed: 1974
Location of Line: Tenterden, Kent to Bodiam, East Sussex
Length of Line: 10½ miles

Nº of Steam Locos: 12
Nº of Other Locos: 6
Nº of Members: 2,504
Annual Membership Fee: £22.00
Approx Nº of Visitors P.A.: 99,000
Gauge: Standard
Web site: www.kesr.org.uk

GENERAL INFORMATION

Nearest Mainline Station: Headcorn (8 miles)
Nearest Bus Station: Tenterden
Car Parking: Free parking available at Tenterden Town and Northiam Stations
Coach Parking: Tenterden & Northiam
Souvenir Shop(s): Yes
Food & Drinks: Yes

SPECIAL INFORMATION

Built as Britain's first light railway, the K&ESR opened in 1900 and was epitomised by sharp curved and steep gradients and to this day retains a charm and atmosphere all of its own.

OPERATING INFORMATION

Opening Times: From March to October and in December. The return journey time is 1 hour 55 minutes. Please phone the 24 hour talking-timetable for precise operating information: (01580) 762943
Steam Working: Every operational day
Prices: Adult Ticket – £11.00
　　　　　 Child Ticket – £6.00
　　　　　 Senior Citizen Ticket – £10.00
　　　　　 Family Ticket – £29.00
Note: The prices shown above are for Day Rover tickets which allow unlimited travel on the day of purchase.

Detailed Directions by Car:
From London and Kent Coast: Travel to Ashford (M20) then take the A28 to Tenterden; From Sussex Coast: Take A28 from Hastings to Northiam.

LAKESIDE & HAVERTHWAITE RAILWAY

Address: Haverthwaite Station, near
Ulverston, Cumbria   LA12 8AL
Telephone Nº: (015395) 31594
Year Formed: 1973
Location of Line: Haverthwaite to
Lakeside
Length of Line: 3½ miles

Nº of Steam Locos: 8
Nº of Other Locos: 6
Nº of Members: 250
Annual Membership Fee: £10.00 Adult,
£5.00 Juniors
Approx Nº of Visitors P.A.: 170,000
Gauge: Standard
Web site: www.lakesiderailway.co.uk

GENERAL INFORMATION

Nearest Mainline Station: Ulverston (7 miles)
Nearest Bus Station: Haverthwaite (100 yards)
Car Parking: Plenty of spaces – £1.50 charge
Coach Parking: Free parking at site
Souvenir Shop(s): Yes
Food & Drinks: Yes

SPECIAL INFORMATION

Connections are available at Lakeside for
Windermere Lake Cruises to Bowness & Ambleside.
Through tickets are available.

OPERATING INFORMATION

Opening Times: Daily from 31st March to 28th
October inclusive. Santa Specials run on 1st, 2nd,
8th, 9th, 15th and 16th of December. Also a Thomas
the Tank Engine weekend on 3rd and 4th November.
Steam Working: Daily from morning to late
afternoon.
Prices: Adult Return £5.20   Single £3.10
Child Return £2.60   Single £2.10
Family Ticket £14.20
Note: Prices vary for Special Events.

Detailed Directions by Car:
From All Parts: Exit the M6 at Junction 36 and follow the brown tourist signs.

THE LAVENDER LINE

Address: Isfield Station, Isfield, near Uckfield, East Sussex TN22 5XB
Telephone Nº: (01825) 750515
Year Formed: 1992
Location of Line: East Sussex between Lewes and Uckfield
Length of Line: 1 mile

Nº of Steam Locos: 2
Nº of Other Locos: 1 + DEMU
Nº of Members: Approximately 400
Annual Membership Fee: £15.00
Approx Nº of Visitors P.A.: 12,500
Gauge: Standard
Web site: www.lavender-line.co.uk

GENERAL INFO

Nearest Mainline Station:
Uckfield (3 miles)
Nearest Bus Station:
Uckfield (3 miles)
Car Parking: Free parking at site
Coach Parking: Can cater for coach parties – please contact the Railway.
Souvenir Shop: Yes
Food & Drinks: Yes – Cinders Buffet

SPECIAL INFO

Isfield Station has been restored as a Southern Railway country station complete with the original L.B.S.C.R. signalbox.

OPERATING INFO

Opening Times:
Sundays throughout the year. Saturdays and Sundays in June, July and August plus Wednesdays and Thursdays in August. Also open on Bank Holidays and in December for Santa Specials.
Steam Working:
Please phone for details.
Prices: Adult £7.00
             Child £5.00
             Senior Citizen £6.00
             Family Ticket £20.00
             (2 adults + 3 children)
All tickets offer unlimited rides on the day of issue and prices may vary on special event days.

Detailed Directions by Car::
From All Parts: Isfield is just off the A26 midway between Lewes and Uckfield.

LINCOLNSHIRE WOLDS RAILWAY

Address: The Railway Station, Ludborough, Lincolnshire   DN36 5SQ
Telephone Nº: (01507) 363881
Year Formed: 1979
Location of Line: Ludborough – off the A16(T) between Grimsby and Louth
Length of Line: 1 mile

Nº of Steam Locos: 1   **Other Locos:** 7
Nº of Members of the Supporting Society (GLRPS): 400+
Annual Membership Fee: £20.00 Family, £10.00 Adult, £6.00 Senior Citizen/Junior
Approx Nº of Visitors P.A.: 7,000
Gauge: Standard

GENERAL INFORMATION

Nearest Mainline Station: Grimsby (8 miles)
Nearest Bus Stop: Ludborough (½ mile)
Car Parking: 100 spaces for cars at the Station
Coach Parking: Space for 1 coach only
Souvenir Shop(s): Yes
Food & Drinks: Yes

SPECIAL INFORMATION

The buildings and facilities at Ludborough have been completed and short steam trips commenced in 1998. A line extension to North Thoresby (1 mile) is currently underway.

OPERATING INFORMATION

Opening Times: Certain Sundays from January to December. Also Santa Specials in December. Advance bookings are essential.
Steam Working: Contact the Railway for details.
Prices: Adults £3.50
Senior Citizens/Children £2.00
Family £8.00 (2 adults + 4 children)
Different fares may apply at Special Events.
Prices include unlimited rides throughout the day.

Web site: www.lincolnshirewoldsrailway.co.uk

Detailed Directions by Car:
The Railway is situated near Ludborough, ½ mile off the A16(T) Louth to Grimsby road. Follow signs to Fulstow to reach the station (approximately ½ mile). Do not turn into Ludborough but stay on the bypass.

LLANGOLLEN RAILWAY

Address: The Station, Abbey Road, Llangollen, Denbighshire LL20 8SN	**N° of Steam Locos:** 14
Telephone N°: (01978) 860979	**N° of Other Locos:** 13
Year Formed: 1975	**N° of Members:** 1,300
Location of Line: Valley of the River Dee from Llangollen to Carrog	**Annual Membership Fee:** Adult £18.00; Family £25.00; Junior (under-16) £10.00
Length of Line: 7½ miles	**Approx N° of Visitors P.A.:** 90,000
	Gauge: Standard

GENERAL INFORMATION

Nearest Mainline Station: Ruabon (6 miles)
Nearest Bus Station: Wrexham (12 miles)
Car Parking: Public car park at Lower Dee Mill off A539 Ruabon road.
Coach Parking: Market Street car park in town centre
Souvenir Shop(s): Yes – at Llangollen Station
Food & Drinks: Yes – at Llangollen, Berwyn, Glyndyfrdwy and Carrog Stations.

SPECIAL INFORMATION

The route originally formed part of the line from Ruabon to Barmouth Junction, closed in 1964. The railway has been rebuilt by volunteers since 1975, reopening to Carrog in 1996.
The ultimate aim is to reopen to Corwen (10 miles).

OPERATING INFORMATION

Opening Times: Services run daily from 28th April to 4th November. Also on weekends in December, other Santa Specials near Christmas and a number of other dates throughout the year including most days in April.
Steam Working: Phone the Talking timetable number for further details: (01978) 860951
Prices: Adult Return £8.00 (Llangollen to Carrog)
Child Return £4.00
Family £18.00 (2 adults + 2 children)
Senior Citizens £6.00
Note: Shorter journeys are cheaper.

Web Site: www.llangollen-railway.co.uk

Detailed Directions by Car:
From South & West: Go via the A5 to Llangollen. At the traffic lights turn into Castle Street to the River bridge; From North & East: Take the A483 to A539 junction and then via Trefor to Llangollen River bridge. The Station is adjacent to the River Dee.

MANGAPPS RAILWAY MUSEUM

Address: Southminster Road, Burnham-on-Crouch, Essex CM0 8QQ	**Nº of Steam Locos:** 6
Telephone Nº: (01621) 784898	**Nº of Other Locos:** 10
Year Formed: 1989	**Nº of Members:** –
Location of Line: Mangapps Farm	**Annual Membership Fee:** –
Length of Line: ¾ mile	**Approx Nº of Visitors P.A.:** 20,000
	Gauge: Standard

GENERAL INFORMATION

Nearest Mainline Station: Burnham-on-Crouch (1 mile)
Nearest Bus Station: –
Car Parking: Ample free parking at site
Coach Parking: Ample free parking at site
Souvenir Shop(s): Yes
Food & Drinks: Yes – drinks and snacks only

SPECIAL INFORMATION

The Railway endeavours to recreate the atmosphere of an East Anglian light railway. It also includes an extensive museum with an emphasis on East Anglian items and signalling.

Web Site: www.mangapps.co.uk

OPERATING INFORMATION

Opening Times: Closed during January and November, then open every weekend and bank holiday (except over Christmas). Open every day during the August School Holidays and for a number of other special events throughout the year. Santa Specials run during weekends in December. Please contact the railway for further details.
Steam Working: Bank Holiday Sundays and Mondays plus certain other dates. Diesel at other times. Please contact the railway for further details.
Prices: Adult – Steam £6.00; Diesel £5.00
Child – Steam £3.00; Diesel £2.50
Senior Citizen – Steam £5.00; Diesel £4.00
Note: Prices for special events may differ.

Detailed Directions by Car:
From South & West: From M25 take either the A12 or A127 and then the A130 to Rettendon Turnpike and then follow signs to Burnham; From North: From A12 take A414 to Oak Corner then follow signs to Burnham.

THE MIDDLETON RAILWAY

Address: The Station, Moor Road, Hunslet, Leeds LS10 2JQ	**N° of Steam Locos:** 15
Telephone N°: (0113) 271-0320	**N° of Other Locos:** 12
Year Formed: 1960	**Annual Membership Fee:** Adults £12.00
Location of Line: Moor Road to Middleton Park	**Approx N° of Visitors P.A.:** 20,000
Length of Line: 1½ miles	**Gauge:** Standard
	Web Site: www.middletonrailway.org.uk

GENERAL INFORMATION

Nearest Mainline Station: Leeds City (1 mile)
Nearest Bus Station: Leeds (1½ miles)
Car Parking: Free parking at site
Coach Parking: Free parking at site
Souvenir Shop(s): Yes
Food & Drinks: Yes

SPECIAL INFORMATION

Operating in every year since 1758, the railway still operates under its original Act of Parliament. Passenger services run from the station into Middleton Park. A large collection of preserved industrial steam and diesel engines are displayed, many of them more than 100 years old.

OPERATING INFORMATION

Opening Times: Weekends and Bank Holidays from 31st March to Christmas Eve. Also open on Wednesdays in August. Diesel services run at 40 minute intervals from 1.00pm to 4.20pm.
Steam Working: Every Sunday and Bank Holiday Money from 1st April to 27th November. Steam services run at 40 minute intervals from 11.00am to 4.20pm.
Prices: Adult £4.50
　　　　　　 Child £2.50
　　　　　　 Family £12.00
　　　　　　　　　　(2 adults + 3 children)
Tickets provide for unlimited travel on the day of issue.
Please send the railway a SAE for the timetable and details of special events or check the web site.

Detailed Directions by Car:
From the South: Take the M621 Northbound and exit at Junction 5. Turn right at the top of the slip road and take the 3rd exit at the roundabout. The Railway is 50 yards on the right; From the West: Take the M621 Southbound and exit at Junction 6. Turn left at the end of the slip road then left again into Moor Road at the next set of traffic lights. Bear right at the mini roundabout and the railway is on the left after 150 yards.

MID-HANTS RAILWAY (WATERCRESS LINE)

Address: The Railway Station, Alresford, Hampshire SO24 9JG	**Nº of Steam Locos:** 16
Telephone Nº: (01962) 733810 General enquiries; (01962) 734866 Timetable	**Nº of Other Locos:** 8
	Nº of Members: 4,500
Year Formed: 1977	**Annual Membership Fee:** Adult £20.00
Location of Line: Alresford to Alton	**Approx Nº of Visitors P.A.:** 130,000
Length of Line: 10 miles	**Gauge:** Standard
	Web Site: www.watercressline.co.uk

GENERAL INFO

Nearest Mainline Station: Alton (adjacent) or Winchester (7 miles)
Nearest Bus Station: Winchester or Alton
Car Parking: Pay and display at Alton and Alresford Stations (Alresford free on Sundays & Bank Holidays)
Coach Parking: By arrangement at Alresford Station
Souvenir Shop(s): At Alresford, Ropley & Alton
Food & Drinks: Yes – Buffet on most trains. 'West Country' buffet at Alresford

SPECIAL INFO

The railway runs through four fully restored stations and has a Loco yard and picnic area at Ropley.

OPERATING INFO

Opening Times: Weekends and Bank Holidays from January to October. Weekdays from May to September and during School Holidays. Santa Specials run at weekends and on other dates in December.
Steam Working: All operating days although a Steam/DMU combination is sometimes in service.
Prices: Adult £10.00
          Child (ages 2 to 16) £5.00
          Senior Citizens £10.00
          Family £25.00
          (2 adults + 2 children)
A discount is available for pre-booked parties of 15 or more people. Write or call for a booking form.

Detailed Directions by Car:
From the East: Take the M25 then A3 and A31 to Alton; From the West: Exit the M3 at Junction 9 and take the A31 to Alresford Station.

MID-NORFOLK RAILWAY

Address: The Railway Station,
Station Road, Dereham   NR19 1DF
Telephone Nº: (01362) 690633 or 851723
Year Formed: 1995
Location: East Dereham to Wymondham
Length of Line: 11 miles
Web site: www.mnr.org.uk

Nº of Steam Locos: Visiting locos only
Nº of Other Locos: 7
Nº of Members: 1,000
Annual Membership Fee: £15.00
Approx Nº of Visitors P.A.: 14,000
Gauge: Standard

GENERAL INFORMATION

Nearest Mainline Station: Wymondham (1 mile)
Nearest Bus Station: Wymondham or East
Dereham – each ½ mile away
Car Parking: Available at Dereham Station
Coach Parking: Available at Dereham Station
Souvenir Shop(s): Yes – at Dereham Station
Food & Drinks: Yes – at Dereham Station

SPECIAL INFORMATION

The Mid-Norfolk Railway aims to preserve the
former Great Eastern Railway from Wymondham to
County School. The section from Wymondham to
Dereham was opened to passenger and freight traffic
in May 1999 and clearance work is now complete on
the East Dereham to County School section.

OPERATING INFORMATION

Opening Times: Every Sunday and Bank Holiday
from 18th March to 18th November. Also open on
Saturdays from 17th March to 27th October,
Wednesdays from 9th May to 24th October and
Thursdays from 26th July to 30th August.
Steam Working: Weekends and Bank Holidays
from 12th May to 1st July inclusive with the visiting
Western Region Pannier Tank number 9466.
Prices: Adult Return £6.00 (Diesel)
Child Return £3.00 (Diesel)
Adult Return £10.00 (Steam days)
Child Return £5.00 (Steam days)

Detailed Directions by Car:
From All Parts: From the A47 bypass, turn into Dereham and follow the signs for the Town Centre. Turn right at
the BP Garage – look out for the brown tourist signs – you will see the Station on your right.

MID-SUFFOLK LIGHT RAILWAY MUSEUM

Address: Brockford Station,
Wetheringsett, Suffolk   IP14 5PW
Telephone Nº: (01449) 766899
Year Formed: 1990
Location of Line: Wetheringsett, Suffolk
Length of Line: ¼ mile

Nº of Steam Locos: 2 (1 operational)
Nº of Other Locos: 1
Nº of Members: 350
Annual Membership Fee: £10.00
Approx Nº of Visitors P.A.: 1,750
Gauge: Standard
Web site: www.mslr.org.uk

GENERAL INFORMATION

Nearest Mainline Station: Stowmarket
Nearest Bus Station: Ipswich
Car Parking: Available on site
Coach Parking: Available on site
Souvenir Shop(s): Yes
Food & Drinks: Yes

SPECIAL INFORMATION

The Mid-Suffolk Light Railway served the heart of
the county for 50 years, despite being bankrupt
before the first train ran. In a beautiful rural setting,
the Museum seeks to preserve the memory of a
unique branch line.

OPERATING INFORMATION

Opening Times: Sundays and Bank Holiday
Mondays from Easter to the end of September and
also on Wednesdays in August. Open from 11.00am
to 5.00pm. Special events open at different times.
Steam Working: 8th & 9th April; 6th, 7th, 27th &
28th May; 17th June; 1st July; 5th, 12th, 19th, 26th
& 27th August; 16th & 30th September; 9th, 16th &
30th December. Possibly other dates – contact the
railway or check the web site for details.
Prices: Adult £5.00
       Child £2.50
       Family Ticket £12.50
Tickets allow unlimited travel on the day of issue.

Detailed Directions by Car:
The Museum is situated 14 miles north of Ipswich and 28 miles south of Norwich, just off the A140. Look for
Mendlesham TV mast and then follow the brown tourist signs from the A140.

MIDLAND RAILWAY – BUTTERLEY

Address: Butterley Station, Ripley, Derbyshire DE5 3QZ	**Nº of Steam Locos:** 25
Telephone Nº: (01773) 747674	**Nº of Other Locos:** 53
Year Formed: 1969	**Nº of Members:** 2,000
Location of Line: Butterley, near Ripley	**Annual Membership Fee:** £16.00
Length of Line: Standard gauge 3½ miles, Narrow gauge 0.8 mile	**Approx Nº of Visitors P.A.:** 130,000
	Gauge: Standard, various Narrow gauges and miniature

GENERAL INFORMATION

Nearest Mainline Station: Alfreton (6 miles)
Nearest Bus Station: Bus stop outside Butterley Station.
Car Parking: Free parking at site – ample space
Coach Parking: Free parking at site
Souvenir Shop(s): Yes – at Butterley and Swanwick
Food & Drinks: Yes – both sites + bar on train

SPECIAL INFORMATION

The Centre is a unique project with a huge Museum development together with narrow gauge, miniature & model railways as well as a country park and farm park. Includes an Award-winning Victorian Railwayman's church and Princess Royal Class Locomotive Trust Depot.

OPERATING INFORMATION

Opening Times: The centre is open daily – trains do not run every day it is open however.
Steam Working: Weekends and bank holidays throughout the year and most days in the school holidays. Phone for further details. 'Day Out With Thomas' 2007 events: 26th May to 3rd June; 4th to 12th August; 13th & 14th October; 27th to 30th December.
Prices: Adult £9.95
        Children £5.00
        Senior Citizens £8.95
Note: Supplements are charged for some special events.

Detailed Directions by Car:
From All Parts: From the M1 exit at Junction 28 and take the A38 towards Derby. The Centre is signposted at the junction with the B6179.

NENE VALLEY RAILWAY

Address: Wansford Station, Stibbington, Peterborough PE8 6LR	**N° of Steam Locos:** 17
Telephone N°: (01780) 784444 enquiries; (01780) 784404 talking timetable	**N° of Other Locos:** 11
Year Formed: 1977	**N° of Members:** 1,300
Location: Off A1 to west of Peterborough	**Annual Membership Fee:** Adult £14.00; Child £8.00; Joint £21.50; OAP £8.00
Length of Line: 7½ miles	**Approx N° of Visitors P.A.:** 65,000
	Gauge: Standard

GENERAL INFORMATION

Nearest Mainline Station: Peterborough (¾ mile)
Nearest Bus Station: Peterborough (Queensgate – ¾ mile)
Car Parking: Free parking at Wansford & Orton Mere
Coach Parking: Free coach parking at Wansford
Souvenir Shop(s): Yes
Food & Drinks: Yes

SPECIAL INFORMATION

The railway is truly international in flavour with British and Continental locomotives and rolling stock.

Web site: www.nvr.org.uk

OPERATING INFORMATION

Opening Times: Most weekends from February to October. Mid-week on various dates from May to the end of August and also at various other times. Santa Specials run in December. Contact the Railway for further details. Open 9.00am to 4.30pm.
Steam Working: Most services are steam hauled apart from on diesel days and times of high fire risk.
Prices: Adult £10.50 (Special events £13.00)
Child £5.50 (age 3-15) (Special events £6.50)
Family £26.00 (2 adult + 3 child) (Special £32.00)
Senior Citizens/Disabled £8.00 (Special £10.00)

Detailed Directions by Car:
The railway is situated off the southbound carriageway of the A1 between the A47 and A605 junctions – west of Peterborough and south of Stamford.

NORTHAMPTON & LAMPORT RAILWAY

Address: Pitsford & Bramford Station, Pitsford Road, Chapel Brampton, Northampton NN6 8BA	**N° of Steam Locos:** 5
	N° of Other Locos: 10
	N° of Members: 600
Telephone N°: (01604) 820327 (infoline)	**Annual Membership Fee:** £10.00
Year Formed: 1983 (became operational in November 1995)	**Approx N° of Visitors P.A.:** 20,000
	Gauge: Standard
Length of Line: 1¼ miles at present	**Web site:** www.nlr.org.uk

GENERAL INFORMATION

Nearest Mainline Station: Northampton (5 miles)
Nearest Bus Station: Northampton (5 miles)
Car Parking: Free parking at site
Coach Parking: Free parking at site
Souvenir Shop(s): Yes
Food & Drinks: Yes

SPECIAL INFORMATION

A developing railway – this became operational again on 18th November 1995.

OPERATING INFORMATION

Opening Times: Sundays and Bank holidays from March to October. Santa Specials in December. Open 10.30am to 5.00pm though the last train runs at 3.45pm.

Steam Working: Generally between April and September and also in December.

Prices: Adult £3.80
Child £2.80
Family £11.00 (2 adults + 2 children)
Senior Citizen £2.80

Fares may vary on Special Event days.

Detailed Directions by Car:
The station is situated along the Pitsford road at Chapel Brampton, approximately 5 miles north of Northampton. Heading north out of town, it is signposted to the right on the A5199 (A50) Welford Road at Chapel Brampton crossroads or on the left on the A508 Market Harborough road at the Pitsford turn.

NORTH NORFOLK RAILWAY

Address: Sheringham Station, Sheringham, Norfolk   NR26 8RA
Telephone Nº: (01263) 820800
Year Formed: 1975
Location of Line: Sheringham to Holt via Weybourne
Length of Line: 5½ miles

Nº of Steam Locos: 5
Nº of Other Locos: 4
Nº of Members: 1,600
Annual Membership Fee: £17.00
Approx Nº of Visitors P.A.: 130,000
Gauge: Standard
Web site: www.nnr.co.uk

GENERAL INFORMATION

Nearest Mainline Station: Sheringham (200 yards)
Nearest Bus Station: Outside the Station
Car Parking: Adjacent to Sheringham and Holt
Coach Parking: Adjacent to Sheringham and Holt
Souvenir Shop(s): At Sheringham Station
Food & Drinks: Yes – main catering facilities at Sheringham Station. Light refreshments elsewhere.

SPECIAL INFORMATION

William Marriott Railway Museum opened at Holt Station in Summer 2006. The line was once part of the Midland & Great Northern Joint Railway.

OPERATING INFORMATION

Opening Times: Most days from mid-March to the end of October plus Santa Specials in December.
Special Events: Steam Galas on 31st August to 2nd September + 31st December to 2nd January; Beer Festival 13th to 15th July, 1940s Weekend 15th & 16th September.
Steam Working: 10.30am to 4.30pm
Prices: Adult £9.50
　　　　　Child £6.00   (Under 5's free of charge)
　　　　　Family £29.00 (includes free brochure)
　　　　　Senior Citizens £8.50
All the above prices are all-day Rover tickets.

Detailed Directions by Car:
Sheringham Station is situated just off the A149. Holt Station is located at High Kelling, just off the A148.

NORTH TYNESIDE STEAM RAILWAY

Address: Stephenson Railway Museum, Middle Engine Lane, North Shields, NE29 8DX	**N⁰ of Steam Locos:** 5
	N⁰ of Other Locos: 3
	N⁰ of Members: None
Telephone N⁰: (0191) 200-7146	**Annual Membership Fee:** £9.00
Year Formed: 1986	**Approx N⁰ of Visitors P.A.:** 30,000
Location: Stephenson Railway Museum	**Gauge:** Standard
Length of Line: 1½ miles	**Web site:** www.ntsra.org.uk

GENERAL INFORMATION

Nearest Mainline Station: Newcastle Central (5 miles)
Nearest Bus Station: North Shields
Car Parking: Free parking available on site
Coach Parking: Free parking available on site
Souvenir Shop(s): No
Food & Drinks: On major event days only

SPECIAL INFORMATION

A programme of events and activities is available from the Museum on request.

OPERATING INFORMATION

Opening Times: Weekends and daily during School Holidays from May to October, 11.00am to 4.00pm
Steam Working: Sundays and Bank Holiday Mondays from June to September.
Prices: Adult Return £2.00
Child Return £1.00
Family Return £5.00

Detailed Directions by Car:
The Railway is adjacent to the Silverlink Retail Park approximately ½ mile from the junction between the A19 and A1058. From the A19/A1058 junction look for the signs for 'Silverlink' before following the Brown tourist signs to the Stephenson Railway Museum.

NORTH YORKSHIRE MOORS RAILWAY

Address: Pickering Station, Pickering, North Yorkshire YO18 7AJ	**N° of Steam Locos:** 20
Telephone N°: (01751) 472508 (enquiries)	**N° of Other Locos:** 12
Year Formed: 1967	**N° of Members:** 8,000
Location of Line: Pickering to Grosmont and Whitby via stations at Levisham and Goathland	**Annual Membership Fee:** Adult £16.00; Over 60's £12.00
Length of Line: 18 miles	**Approx N° of Visitors P.A.:** 300,000
	Gauge: Standard
	Web site: www.nymr.co.uk

GENERAL INFORMATION

Nearest Mainline Station: Grosmont (adjacent to the NYMR station) or Whitby

Nearest Bus Station: Pickering (½ mile)

Car Parking: Available at each station

Coach Parking: Available at Pickering & Grosmont

Souvenir Shop(s): Yes – at Pickering, Goathland, and Grosmont Stations plus Grosmont MPD

Food & Drinks: Pickering, Grosmont & Goathland

SPECIAL INFORMATION

The NYMR runs through the spectacular North Yorkshire Moors National Park and is the most popular in the country. As seen in 'Heartbeat' and the first Harry Potter film. The railway now operates regular services to and from Whitby.

OPERATING INFORMATION

Opening Times: Open daily from 17th March to 4th November plus some other Winter dates and Santa Specials in December.

Steam Working: Usually daily – please phone the Railway for timetable information

Prices: Adult £14.00 (all-day travel)
Child £7.00 (all-day travel)
Family Tickets £30.00
(2 adults and up to 4 children)

Detailed Directions by Car:

From the South: Follow the A64 past York to the Malton bypass then take the A169 to Pickering; From the North: Take A171 towards Whitby then follow the minor road through Egton to Grosmont.

NOTTINGHAM TRANSPORT HERITAGE CENTRE

Address: Nottingham Transport Heritage Centre, Mere Way, Ruddington, Nottingham NG11 6NX **Telephone Nº:** (0115) 940-5705 **Fax Nº:** (0115) 940-5905 **Year Formed:** 1990 (Opened in 1994) **Location of Line:** Ruddington to Loughborough Junction	**Length of Line:** 9 miles **Nº of Steam Locos:** 6 **Nº of Other Locos:** 7 **Nº of Members:** 850 **Annual Membership Fee:** £12.00 **Approx Nº of Visitors P.A.:** 15,000 **Gauge:** Standard **Web site:** www.nthc.co.uk

GENERAL INFORMATION

Nearest Mainline Station: Nottingham (5 miles)
Nearest Bus Station: Bus service from Nottingham to the Centre
Car Parking: Free parking at site
Coach Parking: Free parking at site
Souvenir Shop(s): Yes
Food & Drinks: Yes

SPECIAL INFORMATION

The Heritage Centre covers an area of over eleven acres and is set within the Rushcliffe Country Park in Ruddington. Trains run to Rushcliffe Halt.

OPERATING INFORMATION

Opening Times: Sundays and Bank Holidays from April until early October. Open 10.45am to 5.00pm. Also open for Santa Specials on December weekends.
Steam Working: Steam service runs from 11.30am
Prices: Adult £6.00
Child £3.00
Senior Citizens £5.00
Family £17.00 (2 adults + 3 children)

Detailed Directions by Car:
From All Parts: The centre is situated off the A60 Nottingham to Loughborough Road and is signposted just south of the traffic lights at Ruddington.

PAIGNTON & DARTMOUTH STEAM RAILWAY

Address: Queen's Park Station, Torbay Road, Paignton TQ4 6AF	**Nº of Steam Locos:** 6
Telephone Nº: (01803) 555872	**Nº of Other Locos:** 3
Year Formed: 1973	**Nº of Members:** –
Location of Line: Paignton to Kingswear	**Annual Membership Fee:** –
Length of Line: 7 miles	**Approx Nº of Visitors P.A.:** 350,000
	Gauge: Standard
	Web site: www.paignton-steamrailway.co.uk

GENERAL INFORMATION

Nearest Mainline Station: Paignton (adjacent)
Nearest Bus Station: Paignton (2 minutes walk)
Car Parking: Multi-storey or Mainline Station
Coach Parking: Multi-storey (3 minutes walk)
Souvenir Shop(s): Yes – at Paignton & Kingswear
Food & Drinks: Yes – at Paignton & Kingswear

SPECIAL INFORMATION

A passenger ferry is available from Kingswear Station across to Dartmouth. Combined excursions are also available including train and river trips.

OPERATING INFORMATION

Opening Times: Open daily from June to September (inclusive). Also open days in April, May, October and December (phone for details).
Steam Working: Trains run throughout the day from 10.30am to 5.00pm.
Prices: Adult Return £9.00 (Includes ferry charge)
Child Return £6.00 (Includes ferry charge)
Family Return £28.00 (2 adults + 2 children)
Note: Cheaper fares are charged for shorter journeys

Detailed Directions by Car:
From All Parts: Take the M5 to Exeter and then the A380 to Paignton.

PALLOT STEAM, MOTOR & GENERAL MUSEUM

Address: Rue de Bechet, Trinity, Jersey, JE3 5BE	**Nº of Steam Locos:** 4
Telephone Nº: (01534) 865307	**Nº of Other Locos:** 2
Year Formed: 1990	**Nº of Members:** None
Location of Line: Trinity, Jersey	**Approx Nº of Visitors P.A.:** 12,000
Length of Line: A third of a mile	**Gauge:** Standard and 2 feet
	Web site: www.pallotmuseum.co.uk

GENERAL INFORMATION

Nearest Mainline Station: None
Nearest Bus Station: St. Helier
Car Parking: Available on site
Coach Parking: Available on site
Souvenir Shop(s): Yes
Food & Drinks: Snacks only

SPECIAL INFORMATION

The museum was founded by Lyndon (Don) Pallot who spent his early career as a trainee engineer with the old Jersey Railway.

OPERATING INFORMATION

Opening Times: Daily from 1st April to 31st October. Open from 10.00am to 5.00pm. Closed on Sundays.
Steam Working: Every Thursday and also on high-season Tuesdays.
Prices: Adult Museum Admission £4.50
Child Museum Admission £1.50
Senior Citizen Museum Admission £4.00
Adult Train Ride £1.50
Child Train Ride £1.00

Detailed Directions by Car:
The museum lies between the A8 and the A9 main roads (Bus Route 5 is easiest) and is signposted off both of these roads.

PEAK RAIL PLC

Address: Matlock Station, Matlock, Derbyshire   DE4 3NA
Telephone Nº: (01629) 580381
Fax Nº: (01629) 760645
Year Formed: 1975
Location of Line: Matlock Riverside to Rowsley South

Length of Line: 4 miles
Nº of Steam Locos: 6   **Other Locos**: 20+
Nº of Members: 1,700
Annual Adult Membership Fee: £16.00
Approx Nº of Visitors P.A.: 40,000
Gauge: Standard
Web site: www.peakrail.co.uk

GENERAL INFO

Nearest Mainline Station: Matlock (500 yards)
Nearest Bus Station: Matlock
Car Parking: Paid car parking at Matlock Station, 200 spaces at Rowsley South Station, 20 spaces at Darley Dale Station
Coach Parking: Free parking at Rowsley South
Souvenir Shop(s): Yes
Food & Drinks: Yes

SPECIAL INFO

The Palatine Restaurant Car is available whilst travelling on the train and caters for Sunday Lunches, Teas and Party Bookings. Coach parties are welcomed when the railway is operating.

OPERATING INFO

Opening Times: Sundays from January to March and in November. Weekends during the rest of the year. Also Wednesdays in June and July, Tuesdays and Wednesdays in August and Wednesdays in the first two weeks of September.
Steam Working: All services throughout the year.
Prices: Adult Return £6.00
          Children – Under-3's Free
          Children – Ages 3-5 £1.00
          Children – Ages 6-15 £3.00
          Senior Citizen Return £4.60
          Family Ticket
          (2 adults + 3 children) £17.00

Detailed Directions by Car:
Exit the M1 at Junctions 28, 29 or 30 and follow signs towards Matlock. From North and South take A6 direct to Matlock. From Stoke-on-Trent, take the A52 to Ashbourne, then the A5035 to Matlock. Upon reaching Matlock follow the brown tourist signs.

PLYM VALLEY RAILWAY

Address: Marsh Mills Station, Coypool Road, Plympton, Plymouth PL7 4NW	**N⁰ of Steam Locos:** 3
Telephone N⁰: (01752) 330881	**N⁰ of Other Locos:** 3
Year Formed: 1980	**N⁰ of Members:** 200
Location of Line: Marsh Mills to World's End, Plympton	**Annual Membership Fee:** £10.00
	Approx N⁰ of Visitors P.A.: 5,000
Length of Line: ½ mile	**Gauge:** Standard
	Web site: www.plymrail.co.uk

GENERAL INFORMATION

Nearest Mainline Station: Plymouth (4 miles)
Nearest Bus Station: Plymouth (3 miles)
Car Parking: Available on site
Coach Parking: Available on site
Souvenir Shop(s): Yes
Food & Drinks: Light snacks available

SPECIAL INFORMATION

The ultimate aim of the railway is to rebuild a 1¼ mile section of the ex-Great Western branch line which ran from Tavistock Junction, just outside of Plymouth, through to Launceston. The section to be rebuilt runs from Marsh Mills to Plym Bridge.

OPERATING INFORMATION

Opening Times: Open for static viewing on most Sundays from 11.00am to 5.00pm. Trains run on the second Sunday in every month from April to November and also the fourth Sunday of the month from June to September. Trains run between 1.00pm to 4.00pm on these dates.

Steam Working: Please contact the railway for further details.

Prices: Adult Return £1.50
　　　　　Child Return 75p

Note: There is no charge to visit the station.

Detailed Directions by Car:
Leave the A38 at the Marsh Mills turn-off and take the B3416 towards Plympton. Turn left into Coypool Road just after the McDonalds restaurant. From Plymouth City Centre, take the A374 to Marsh Mills, then as above.

PONTYPOOL & BLAENAVON RAILWAY

Address: 13a Broad Street, Blaenavon, Torfaen NP4 9ND	**Nº of Steam Locos**: 9
e-mail: info@pbrly.co.uk	**Nº of Other Locos**: 7 + 3 DMUs
Telephone Nº: (01495) 792263	**Nº of Members**: 200
Year Formed: 1980 (Opened 1983)	**Annual Membership Fee**: £12.00
Location of Line: Just off the B4248 between Blaenavon and Brynmawr	**Approx Nº of Visitors P.A.**: 5,700
Length of Line: ¾ mile	**Gauge**: Standard
	Web site: www.pontypool-and-blaenavon.co.uk

GENERAL INFORMATION

Nearest Mainline Station: Abergavenny (5 miles)
Nearest Bus Station: Blaenavon Town (1½ miles) – regular bus service within ¼ mile (except Sundays)
Car Parking: Free parking for 50 cars on site
Coach Parking: Available on site
Souvenir Shop(s): Yes – on the train and also a shop at 13 Broad Street, Blaenavon
Food & Drinks: Light refreshments on the train

SPECIAL INFORMATION

The railway operates over very steep gradients, is run entirely by volunteers and is the highest standard gauge preserved railway in England and Wales.

OPERATING INFORMATION

Opening Times: Every weekend and Bank Holiday Monday from Easter to the end of September. Santa Specials and other Special events also run. Please phone the Railway for details or check the web site.
Steam Working: No steaming at present – services are worked by Diesel locos or DMU.
Prices: Adult £2.50 (unlimited travel
  Child £1.50 on the day of issue
  Family £6.50 with ordinary returns)
Fares and conditions can vary for Special Events.

Detailed Directions by Car:
From All Parts: The railway is situated just off the B4248 between Blaenavon and Brynmawr and is well signposted as you approach Blaenavon. Use Junction 25A if using the M4 from the East, or Junction 26 from the West. Head for Pontypool. From the Midlands use the M50, A40 then A465 to Brynmawr. From North & West Wales consider using the 'Heads of the Valleys' A465 to Brynmawr. As you approach the Railway, look out for the Colliery water tower – you can't miss it!

RAILWAY PRESERVATION SOCIETY OF IRELAND

Address: Castleview, Whitehead,
Co. Antrim, Northern Ireland BT38 9NA
Telephone Nº: (028) 2826-0803
Year Formed: 1964
Location of Line: Whitehead, Co. Antrim
Length of Line: ¼ mile
Gauge: Irish Standard

Nº of Steam Locos: 9
Nº of Other Locos: 5
Nº of Members: 1,100
Annual Membership Fee: Adult £25.00;
Senior £20.00; Junior £15.00; Family £60.00
Approx Nº of Visitors P.A.: 10,000
Web Site: www.rpsi-online.org
E-mail: rpsitrains@hotmail.com

GENERAL INFORMATION

Nearest NIR Station: Whitehead (½ mile)
Nearest Bus Station: Whitehead (½ mile)
Car Parking: Free parking at site
Coach Parking: Free parking at site
Souvenir Shop(s): Yes
Food & Drinks: Yes

SPECIAL INFORMATION

The Society is the only Main Line Steam Operator in Ireland.

OPERATING INFORMATION

Opening Times: Sundays in the Summer and also during Easter and Christmas. There is also a regular timetable of main line excursions. Phone for further details.
Steam Working: 2.00pm to 5.00pm at Whitehead
Prices: Depends on the event or the destination of main line excursions

---

Detailed Directions by Car:
Whitehead is situated about 15 miles to the North of Belfast just off the A2 between Larne and Carrickfergus. The location is clearly signposted in Whitehead.

RIBBLE STEAM RAILWAY

Address: Chain Caul Road, Preston, PR2 2PD
Telephone Nº: (01772) 728800
Year Formed: 1972 (at Southport)
Location: West of Preston City Centre
Length of Line: 3 mile round trip

Nº of Steam Locos: 22
Nº of Other Locos: 21
Nº of Members: 400
Annual Membership Fee: £12.00
Approx Nº of Visitors P.A.: 20,000+
Gauge: Standard
Web site: www.ribblesteam.org.uk

GENERAL INFORMATION

Nearest Mainline Station: Preston (2 miles)
Nearest Bus Station: Preston (2 miles)
Car Parking: Available on site
Coach Parking: Available on site
Souvenir Shop(s): Yes
Food & Drinks: Available

SPECIAL INFORMATION

The Railway's timetable is governed by High Tide on the River Ribble. This is because the line traverses a swing bridge across the Marina entrance – the only preserved steam line to have such a feature!

OPERATING INFORMATION

Opening Times: Open 10.30am to 5.00pm on weekends and Bank Holidays from 31st March to 30th September. Also open on Sundays in October and for Santa specials in December. Please contact the railway for further details.
Steam Working: On all days when the railway is open to the public. Trains run hourly from 11.00am to 4.00pm.
Prices: Adult Return £5.00
         Child Return £3.25
         Family Return £14.00
Note: Different prices may apply for Special Events.

Detailed Directions by Car:
From All Parts: The Railway is located on the Riversway/Docklands Business and Residential Park, just off the A583 Lytham/Blackpool road and approximately 1½ miles to the west of Preston City Centre. Follow the Brown Tourist signs from the A583 for the railway.

ROYAL DEESIDE RAILWAY

Address: Milton of Crathes, Crathes, Banchory, Kincardineshire
Telephone Nº: (01224) 782479
Year Formed: 1996
Location of Line: Milton of Crathes
Length of Line: ¼ mile

Nº of Steam Locos: 1 (from August 2007)
Nº of Other Locos: 2
Nº of Members: 250
Annual Membership Fee: £15.00
Approx Nº of Visitors P.A.: 3,000
Gauge: Standard
Web site: www.deeside-railway.co.uk

GENERAL INFORMATION

Nearest Mainline Station: Aberdeen (14 miles)
Nearest Bus Station: Stagecoach Bluebird bus stop nearby on A93.
Car Parking: Free parking available on site
Coach Parking: Free parking available on site
Souvenir Shop(s): Yes – inside a static carriage
Food & Drinks: Yes – inside a static carriage

SPECIAL INFORMATION

The railway has now commenced diesel-hauled brake-van trips on the ¼ mile of track so far relaid. It is hoped that the steam loco 'Bon Accord' will be in use from August 2007.

OPERATING INFORMATION

Opening Times: A Café with light refreshments, shop and display is located in a static carriage and opens Saturday and Sunday afternoons 1.00pm to 5.00pm from May to September. Brake van trips now run on Sunday afternoons from May to September 2.00pm to 4.30pm
Steam Working: Provisionally, from August 2007.
Prices: Please phone the railway for details.

Detailed Directions by Car:
From the South: Take the A90 to Stonehaven. Exit onto the B979 for Stonehaven and follow into the town square. Turn left at the traffic lights and follow signs for the A957 to Banchory (Historic Slug Road). Follow this road for 14 mile via Durris to Crathes and the junction with the A93. Turn left and follow the Brown Tourist signs, turning left for the railway after approximately 600 yards; From the North & West: Follow the A980 to Banchory and turn left onto the A93. Turn right following the Brown Tourist signs for the railway.

RUTLAND RAILWAY MUSEUM

Address: Cottesmore Iron Ore Mines Siding, Ashwell Road, Cottesmore, Oakham, Rutland   LE15 7BX
Telephone Nº: (01572) 813203
Year Formed: 1979
Location of Line: Between the villages of Cottesmore and Ashwell

Length of Line: ¾ mile
Nº of Steam Locos: 13
Nº of Other Locos: 15
Nº of Members: 275
Annual Membership Fee: £10.00
Approx Nº of Visitors P.A.: 8,000
Gauge: Standard

GENERAL INFORMATION

Nearest Mainline Station: Oakham (4 miles)
Nearest Bus Station: Cottesmore/Ashwell (1½ miles)
Car Parking: Available at the site
Coach Parking: Limited space available
Souvenir Shop(s): On open days
Food & Drinks: On open days

SPECIAL INFORMATION

This Industrial Railway Heritage centre is located at the end of the former Ashwell-Cottesmore mineral branch and is based at the former exchange sidings.

Web site: www.rutlandrailwaymuseum.org.uk

OPERATING INFORMATION

Opening Times: Sundays 11.00am to 4.00pm from Easter to the end of September for static viewing. Also Thursday afternoons during this period.
Steam Working: 8th/9th April; 6th//7th/27th/28th May; 17th June; 1st/15th/29th July; 12th/26th/27th August; 9th September; 6th/7th October; 9th/16th/23rd December. Please contact the railway for further details of these events. Pre-booked Driver experience days are also available.
Prices: Adult £4.00
        Child £3.00 (no charge for under 5's)
        Family £12.00
Prices are for admission to the site on steam operating days only. Admission is free at other times. Special prices apply to Santa Specials in December.

Detailed Directions by Car:
From All Parts: The Museum is situated 4 miles north of Oakham between Ashwell and Cottesmore. Follow the brown tourist signs from the B668 Oakham to A1 road or the signs from the A606 Stamford to Oakham Road.

SCOTTISH INDUSTRIAL RAILWAY CENTRE

Address: Dunaskin Open Air Museum, Waterside, Patna, Ayrshire KA6 7JF	**Nº of Steam Locos:** 9
Telephone Nº: (01292) 313579 (Evenings & Weekends)	**Nº of Other Locos:** 26
	Nº of Members: 180
Year Formed: 1974	**Annual Membership Fee:** £10.00
Location of Line: Dunaskin Ironworks	**Approx Nº of Visitors P.A.:** 3,500
Length of Line: A third of a mile	**Gauge:** Standard
	Web site: www.arpg.org.uk

GENERAL INFORMATION

Nearest Mainline Station: Ayr (10 miles)
Nearest Bus Station: ½ hourly bus service from Ayr – phone (01292) 613500 for more information
Car Parking: Free parking available at the site
Coach Parking: Free parking available at the site
Souvenir Shop(s): Yes
Food & Drinks: Cafe on site

SPECIAL INFORMATION

The Railway is located at the former Dunaskin Heritage Centre which unfortunately closed in 2006.

OPERATING INFORMATION

Opening Times: Following the unexpected closure of the Dunaskin Heritage Centre, the railway hopes to be able to resume operation in July 2007 but please check the web site for the latest information.
Steam Working: As above.
Prices: Adult £2.50
Child £2.00
Family Tickets £7.00

Detailed Directions by Car:
From All Parts: Dunaskin Open Air Museum is located adjacent to the A713 Ayr to Castle Douglas road.

SEVERN VALLEY RAILWAY

Address: Railway Station, Bewdley, Worcestershire DY12 1BG	**N° of Steam Locos:** 27
Telephone N°: (01299) 403816	**N° of Other Locos:** 12
Year Formed: 1965	**N° of Members:** 13,000
Location of Line: Kidderminster (Worcs.) to Bridgnorth (Shropshire)	**Annual Membership Fee:** Adult £15.00
Length of Line: 16 miles	**Approx N° of Passengers P.A.:** 248,000
	Gauge: Standard
	Web site: www.svr.co.uk

GENERAL INFORMATION

Nearest Mainline Station: Kidderminster (adjacent)
Nearest Bus Station: Kidderminster (500 yards)
Car Parking: Large car park at Kidderminster. Spaces also available at other stations.
Coach Parking: At Kidderminster
Souvenir Shop(s): At Kidderminster & Bridgnorth
Food & Drinks: Yes – on most trains. Also at Kidderminster, Bewdley and Bridgnorth

SPECIAL INFORMATION

The SVR has numerous special events including an Autumn Steam Gala, 1940's weekend, Classic Car & Bike Day and visits by Thomas the Tank Engine and Santa!

OPERATING INFORMATION

Opening Times: Weekends throughout the year. Also daily from 5th May to 30th September and during local School Holidays.
Steam Working: Train times vary depending on timetable information. Phone for details.
Prices: Vary depending on the journey taken:
Family Day Rover £32.00
(2 adults + 4 children)

Detailed Directions by Car:
For Kidderminster take M5 and exit Junction 3 or Junction 6. Follow the brown tourist signs for the railway; From the South: Take the M40 then M42 to Junction 1 for the A448 from Bromsgrove to Kidderminster.

SOUTH DEVON RAILWAY

Address: Buckfastleigh Station, Buckfastleigh, Devon TQ11 0DZ	**Nº of Steam Locos:** 16
Telephone Nº: (0845) 345-1427	**Nº of Other Locos:** 7
Year Formed: 1969	**Nº of Members:** 1,300
Location of Line: Totnes to Buckfastleigh via Staverton	**Annual Membership Fee:** £14.00
	Approx Nº of Visitors P.A.: 80,000
Length of Line: 7 miles	**Gauge:** Standard
	Web Site: www.southdevonrailway.org

GENERAL INFORMATION

Nearest Mainline Station: Totnes (¼ mile)
Nearest Bus Station: Totnes (½ mile), Buckfastleigh (Station Road)
Car Parking: Free parking at Buckfastleigh, Council/BR parking at Totnes
Coach Parking: As above
Souvenir Shop(s): Yes – Buckfastleigh & on train
Food & Drinks: Yes – at Buckfastleigh & on train

SPECIAL INFORMATION

The railway was opened in 1872 as the Totnes, Buckfastleigh & Ashburton Railway.

OPERATING INFORMATION

Opening Times: Daily from 24th March to 28th October. Also Santa Specials in December.
Steam Working: Almost all trains are steam hauled.
Prices: Adult £9.00
        Child £5.40
        Family £26.00 (2 adults + 2 children)
        Senior Citizen £8.10
Note: Extra discounts are available for large groups.

Detailed Directions by Car:
Buckfastleigh is half way between Exeter and Plymouth on the A38 Devon Expressway. Totnes can be reached by taking the A385 from Paignton and Torquay. Brown tourist signs give directions for the railway.

SPA VALLEY RAILWAY

Address: West Station, Tunbridge Wells, Kent TN2 5QY	**Nº of Steam Locos**: 8
Telephone Nº: (01892) 537715	**Nº of Other Locos**: 9
Year Formed: 1985	**Nº of Members**: Approximately 660
Location of Line: Tunbridge Wells West to Birchden Junction on Gala days	**Annual Membership Fee**: £15.00
	Approx Nº of Visitors P.A.: 30,000
	Gauge: Standard
Length: 3½ miles (4½ miles on Gala days)	**Web Site**: www.spavalleyrailway.co.uk

GENERAL INFORMATION

Nearest Mainline Station: Tunbridge Wells Central (½ mile)

Nearest Bus Stop: Outside Sainsbury's (100yds)

Car Parking: Available nearby

Coach Parking: Coach station in Montacute Road (150 yards)

Souvenir Shop(s): Yes

Food & Drinks: Yes

SPECIAL INFORMATION

The Railway's Tunbridge Wells Terminus is in a historic and unique L.B. & S.C.R. engine shed. The Railway's aims are to extend to Eridge to connect with the Main Line.

OPERATING INFORMATION

Opening Times: Weekends from Easter until 28th October. Some weekdays during School Holidays and also Santa Specials during December.

Steam Working: Most services are steam-hauled. Trains run from 10.30am to 5.00pm (11.00am to 3.30pm midweek and during low season).

Prices: Adult Return £5.00
Child/Senior Citizen Return £4.00
Concessionary Return £4.50
Family Return £15.00 (2 adult + 2 child)

Discounts are available for groups of 20 or more. Fares vary on some special event days. Fares allow unlimited travel on the day of issue except for special event days.

Detailed Directions by Car:

The Spa Valley Railway is in the southern part of Tunbridge Wells, 100 yards off the A26. Station is adjacent to Sainsbury's and Homebase. Car Parks are nearby in Major Yorks Road, Union House & Linden Close.

STEAM – MUSEUM OF THE GREAT WESTERN RAILWAY

Address: STEAM – Museum of the Great Western Railway, Kemble Drive, Swindon   SN2 2TA
Telephone Nº: (01793) 466646
Year Formed: 2000

Nº of Steam Locos: 6
Nº of Other Locos: 1
Approx Nº of Visitors P.A.: 100,000
Web site: www.swindon.gov.uk/steam

GENERAL INFORMATION
Nearest Mainline Station: Swindon (10 min. walk)
Nearest Bus Station: Swindon (10 minute walk)
Car Parking: Ample parking space available in the Outlet Centre (charges apply)
Coach Parking: Free parking on site
Souvenir Shop(s): Yes
Food & Drinks: Yes

SPECIAL INFORMATION
STEAM tells the story of the men and women who built the Great Western Railway.

OPERATING INFORMATION
Opening Times: Open daily all year round from 10.00am to 5.00pm.
Steam Working: During some special events only – please contact the Museum for details.
Prices: Adult Tickets £5.95
Child Tickets £3.80
Family Tickets £14.70
Senior Citizen Tickets £3.90
Children under 5 are admitted free

Detailed Directions by Car:
Exit the M4 at Junction 16 and follow the brown tourist signs to 'Outlet Centre'. Similarly follow the brown signs from all other major routes.   From the Railway Station: STEAM is a short walk and is accessible through the pedestrian tunnel – entrance by Emlyn Square.

STRATHSPEY STEAM RAILWAY

Address: Aviemore Station, Dalfaber Road, Aviemore, Inverness-shire, PH22 1PY	**Length of Line:** 9½ miles at present
	Gauge: Standard
Telephone Nº: (01479) 810725	**Nº of Steam Locos:** 7
Year Formed: 1971	**Nº of Other Locos:** 10
Location of Line: Aviemore to Boat of Garten and Broomhill, Inverness-shire	**Nº of Members:** 800
	Annual Membership Fee: £18.00
	Approx Nº of Visitors P.A.: 56,000

GENERAL INFORMATION

Nearest Mainline Station: Aviemore – Strathspey trains depart from Platform 3

Nearest Bus Station: Aviemore (600 yds)

Car Parking: Available at all stations

Coach Parking: Available at Aviemore and Boat of Garten Stations

Souvenir Shop(s): Yes – at Aviemore and Boat of Garten Stations

Food & Drinks: Available on Steam trains only (except on Saturdays)

SPECIAL INFORMATION

The railway features in the BBC series 'Monarch of the Glen' and operates from Aviemore Station. In the waiting room, there is a small exhibition about the history of the line between Aviemore & Inverness and about the renovation of the station.

OPERATING INFORMATION

Opening Times: Daily from late May to 30th September. Restricted days in April, May and October and other dates in December. Phone for details. Generally open from 9.30am to 4.30pm.

Steam Working: Most trains are steam-hauled but diesel power is used whenever necessary. Phone the Railway for details.

Prices: Adult Return £9.50
Child Return £4.75
Family Return £24.00
(2 adults + up to 3 children)
Day Rover tickets are available for £12.00

Web site: www.strathspeyrailway.co.uk

Detailed Directions by Car:

For Aviemore Station from South: Take the A9 then B970 and turn left between the railway & river bridges. For Boat of Garten from North; Take the A9 then A938 to Carr Bridge, then B9153 and A95 and follow the signs; From North East: Take A95 to Boat of Garten or Broomhill (3½ miles South from Grantown-on-Spey.

Swanage Railway

Address: Station House, Railway Station, Swanage, Dorset BH19 1HB	**N° of Steam Locos:** 5
Telephone N°: (01929) 425800	**N° of Other Locos:** 5
Year Formed: 1976	**N° of Members:** 4,200
Location of Line: Swanage to Norden	**Annual Membership Fee:** Adult £18.00; Junior/Senior Citizen £12.00; Family 36.00
Length of Line: 6 miles	**Approx N° of Visitors P.A.:** 201,452
Gauge: Standard	(exact figures for 2006)
	Web site: www.swanagerailway.co.uk

GENERAL INFORMATION

Nearest Mainline Station: Wareham (10 miles)
Nearest Bus Station: Swanage Station (adjacent)
Car Parking: Park & Ride at Norden. Public car parks in Swanage (5 minutes walk)
Coach Parking: Available at Norden
Souvenir Shop(s): Yes – at Swanage Station
Food & Drinks: Yes – buffet available on trains and also Swanage Station Buffet and at Norden.

SPECIAL INFORMATION

The railway runs along part of the route of the old Swanage to Wareham railway, opened in 1885.

OPERATING INFORMATION

Opening Times: Weekends throughout the year and daily from Easter to October. Also open on some other dates throughout the year. Open from 9.30am to 5.00pm.
Steam Working: All services are steam-hauled
Prices: Adult Return £7.50 (Day Rover £9.50)
Child Return £5.50 (Day Rover £6.50)
Family Ticket £21.00
Note: Day rover tickets are also available.

Detailed Directions by Car:
Norden Park & Ride Station is situated off the A351 on the approach to Corfe Castle. Swanage Station is situated in the centre of the town, just a few minutes walk from the beach. Take the A351 to reach Swanage.

SWANSEA VALE RAILWAY

Address: Upper Bank Works, Pentrechwyth, Swansea SA1 7DB	**N° of Steam Locos:** 5
Telephone N°: (01792) 461000	**N° of Other Locos:** 5
Year Formed: 1980	**N° of Members:** 150
Location of Line: Six Pit Junction, Llansamlet, Swansea	**Annual Membership Fee:** £12.00
	Approx N° of Visitors P.A.: 5,000
	Gauge: Standard
Length of Line: 2 miles	**Web site:** www.swanseavalerailway.co.uk

GENERAL INFORMATION

Nearest Mainline Station: Llansamlet (¾ mile)
Nearest Bus Station: Swansea Quadrant (3 miles)
Car Parking: 150 spaces available at the site
Coach Parking: 3 spaces available at the site
Souvenir Shop(s): Yes – on the trains
Food & Drinks: Light snacks are available on trains

SPECIAL INFORMATION

Guided tours can be arranged at £1.00 per head to view the shed, old turntable base and ash pit.

OPERATING INFORMATION

Opening Times: Services may be disrupted due to engineering works. Please contact the railway to confirm opening times.
Steam Working: Certain dates only, although most running days in the Summer are Steam days. Contact the railway for more information.
Prices: Adult £3.00
    Child £2.00
    Family £10.00
Pay once – ride all day.
Prices may change for special events.

Detailed Directions by Car:
From the East: Exit the M4 at Junction 44 (Swansea East), follow signs for Llansamlet and Morriston. At the third set of traffic lights turn left and look for the steam loco signs; From the West: Exit the M4 at Junction 45 (Morriston) then follow signs for Llansamlet; From City Centre: Cross the river near Parc Tawe Shopping Centre, follow signs to Llansamlet on A4217 for 3 miles. Pass the Colliers Arms on the left, pass under the main line railway bridge and turn next left.

Swindon & Cricklade Railway

Address: Blunsdon Station, Tadpole Lane, Blunsdon, Swindon, Wilts SN25 2DA	**N° of Steam Locos:** 8
Phone N°: (01793) 771615	**N° of Other Locos:** 7
Year Formed: 1978	**N° of Members:** 700
Location of Line: Blunsdon to Hayes Knoll	**Annual Membership Fee:** £13.50
Length of Line: ¾ mile	**Approx N° of Visitors P.A.:** 15,000
	Gauge: Standard

GENERAL INFORMATION

Nearest Mainline Station: Swindon (5 miles)
Nearest Bus Station: Bus stop at Oakhurst (¾ mile)
Car Parking: Free parking at Blunsdon Station
Coach Parking: Free parking at Blunsdon Station
Souvenir Shop(s): Yes
Food & Drinks: Yes

SPECIAL INFORMATION

The Engine Shed at Hayes Knoll Station is open to the public.

Web site: www.swindon-cricklade-railway.org

OPERATING INFORMATION

Opening Times: The Railway is open every weekend and Bank Holidays for viewing. Santa Specials in December and other various special events throughout the year have Steam train rides. Open 11.00am to 4.00pm.
Steam Working: Every Sunday from Easter until the end of October and certain other dates – contact the railway for further details.
Prices: Adult £3.50
Child £2.50
Family £10.00
Prices are different for special events.

Detailed Directions by Car:
From the M4: Exit the M4 at Junction 15 and follow the A419. After the roundabout by the Little Chef, turn left at the next set of traffic lights towards Blunsdon Stadium and follow the signs: From Cirencester: Follow the A419 to the traffic lights at the top of Blunsdon Hill, then turn right and follow signs for the railway.

TANFIELD RAILWAY

Address: Marley Hill Engine Shed, Old Marley Hill, Gateshead, Tyne & Wear NE16 5ET
Telephone Nº: (0191) 388-7545
Fax Nº: (0191) 387-4784
Year Formed: 1976
Location of Line: Between Sunniside & East Tanfield, Co. Durham

Length of Line: 3 miles
Nº of Steam Locos: 29 Standard, 2 Narrow
Nº Other Locos: 12 Standard, 15 Narrow
Nº of Members: 150
Annual Membership Fee: £8.00
Approx Nº of Visitors P.A.: 40,000
Gauge: Standard and Narrow gauge
Web site: www.tanfield-railway.co.uk

GENERAL INFORMATION

Nearest Mainline Station: Newcastle-upon-Tyne (8 miles)
Nearest Bus St'n: Gateshead Interchange (6 miles)
Car Parking: Spaces for 150 cars at Andrews House and 100 spaces at East Tanfield
Coach Parking: Spaces for 6 or 7 coaches only
Souvenir Shop(s): Yes
Food & Drinks: Yes – light snacks only

SPECIAL INFORMATION

Tanfield Railway is the oldest existing railway in use – it was originally opened in 1725. It also runs beside The Causey Arch, the oldest railway bridge in the world.

OPERATING INFORMATION

Opening Times: Every Sunday & Bank Holiday Monday throughout the year. Also opens on Wednesdays & Thursdays in Summer school holidays. Santa Specials run in December.
Steam Working: Most trains are steam-hauled and run from 11.00am to 4.00pm (11.30am to 3.30pm in the Winter). Trains on Thursdays are diesel-hauled.
Prices: Adult £6.00
Child £3.00 (Under 5's travel free)
Senior Citizen £4.00
Family £15.00 (2 adults + 2 children)

Detailed Directions by Car:
Sunniside Station is off the A6076 Sunniside to Stanley road in Co. Durham. To reach the Railway, leave A1(M), follow signs for Beamish museum at Chester-le-Street then continue to Stanley and follow Tanfield Railway signs.

TELFORD STEAM RAILWAY

Address: The Old Loco Shed, Bridge Road, Horsehay, Telford, Shropshire
Telephone Enquiries: (07765) 858348
Year Formed: 1976
Location: Horsehay & Dawley Station
Length of Line: ½ mile standard gauge, an eighth of a mile 2 foot narrow gauge

Nº of Steam Locos: 5
Nº of Other Locos: 12
Nº of Members: Approximately 220
Annual Membership Fee: £10.00
Approx Nº of Visitors P.A.: 10,000
Web site: www.telfordsteamrailway.co.uk

GENERAL INFORMATION

Nearest Mainline Station: Wellington or Telford Central
Nearest Bus Station: Dawley (1 mile)
Car Parking: Free parking at the site
Coach Parking: Free parking at the site
Souvenir Shop(s): 'Freight Stop Gift Shop'
Food & Drinks: 'The Furnaces' Tea Room

SPECIAL INFORMATION

Telford Steam Railway has both a Standard Gauge and Narrow Gauge line as well as Miniature and Model Railways.

OPERATING INFORMATION

Opening Times: Every Sunday and Bank Holiday between Easter and the end of September. Santa Specials run in December. Open 11.00am to 4.30pm. Also open for static viewing on Saturdays from 7th April to 29th September.
Steam Working: 2 foot gauge on all operating days. Standard gauge on the last Sunday of the month, every Sunday in August and also on Bank Holidays.
Prices: Adult all day tickets £4.00
Child all day tickets £2.00
Family all day tickets £10.00

Detailed Directions by Car:
From All Parts: Exit the M54 at Junction 6, travel south along the A5223 then follow the brown tourist signs for the railway.

TYSELEY LOCOMOTIVE WORKS VISITOR CENTRE

Address: 670 Warwick Road, Tyseley, Birmingham   B11 2HL
Telephone Nº: (0121) 708-4960
Year Formed: 1969
Location of Museum: Tyseley
Length of Line: A third of a mile

Nº of Steam Locos: Varies with visiting Locos and restoration contracts
Nº of Members: Approximately 600
Approx Nº of Visitors P.A.: 5,000
Gauge: Standard
Web site: www.vintagetrains.co.uk

GENERAL INFORMATION

Nearest Mainline Station: Tyseley (5 mins. walk)
Nearest Bus Station: Birmingham. Bus Stop at Reddings Lane – 2 minutes walk (Bus route 37 passes the entrance)
Car Parking: 200 spaces at Railway site
Coach Parking: Space at Railway site
Souvenir Shop(s): Yes
Food & Drinks: None

SPECIAL INFORMATION

The Museum runs a large workshop which produces refurbished locomotives, many for operation on Network Rail Lines.

OPERATING INFORMATION

Opening Times: Bank Holidays and Weekends only. Open from 10.00am to 4.00pm.
Steam Working: The Loco Works operates mainline excursions from the Museum Station and runs the Shakespeare Express from Birmingham to Stratford-upon-Avon on Sundays from July to September.
Prices: Adult £2.50
         Child £1.25
         Family £6.25
Note: The above prices are for entrance to the Visitor Centre only. Train rides on the Shakespeare Express are an additional charge.

Detailed Directions by Car:
From the North: Exit the M6 at Junction 6 and take A41 ring road towards Solihull; From the South: Exit the M42 at Junction 5 and take the A41 towards Birmingham.

VALE OF GLAMORGAN RAILWAY

Address: Barry Island Station, Barry
Island, Vale of Glamorgan   CF62 5TH
Telephone Nº: (01446) 748816
Year Formed: 1979 (1994 on present site)
Location of Line: Barry Island
Length of Line: 3 miles

Nº of Steam Locos: 5 (10 in storage)
Nº of Other Locos: 3
Nº of Members: 300
Annual Membership Fee: £10.00
Approx Nº of Visitors P.A.: 15,000
Gauge: Standard
Web site: www.valeglamrail.co.uk

GENERAL INFORMATION
Nearest Mainline Station: Barry Island (across the platform)
Nearest Bus Station: Outside station
Car Parking: Large car park (300 yards)
Coach Parking: Car park (300 yards)
Souvenir Shop(s): Yes
Food & Drinks: Yes

SPECIAL INFORMATION
The aim of the company is to portray the rich history of railways in South Wales.

OPERATING INFORMATION
Opening Times: Weekends from June until early September. Special events will run at Easter and other times throughout the year. Trains run from 11.00am to 4.00pm. Please contact the railway for further details.
Steam Working: Please contact the railway for dates
Prices: Adult £5.00
Child £3.00
Family £14.00
(2 adults + 2 children)
Note: Prices shown above are for Day Rover tickets.

Detailed Directions by Car:
Exit the M4 at Junction 33 and follow the brown tourist signs for the funfair and beach to Barry Island. The station is situated on the left behind the funfair.

THE WEARDALE RAILWAY

Address: Stanhope Station, Stanhope, Bishop Auckland DL13 2YS	**Nº of Steam Locos:** 2
Telephone Nº: (01388) 526262	**Nº of Other Locos:** 3
Year Formed: 1993	**Nº of Members:** 850
Location: Stanhope to Wolsingham, County Durham	**Approx Nº of Visitors P.A.:** 20,000
Length of Line: 5½ miles at present	**Gauge:** Standard
	Web site: www.weardale-railway.org.uk

GENERAL INFORMATION

Nearest Mainline Station: Bishop Auckland (8½ miles)
Nearest Bus Station: Bishop Auckland (8½ miles)
Car Parking: Available at both Stanhope and Wolsingham Stations
Coach Parking: Available at Wolsingham Station
Souvenir Shop(s): Yes
Food & Drinks: Yes – Signal Box Cafe

SPECIAL INFORMATION

Weardale is in the heart of the Pennines and the railway provides magnificent unspoilt views. The area is known for its footpaths and bridleways and the railway provides a useful base for walks between stations along banks of the beautiful River Wear.

OPERATING INFORMATION

Opening Times: Daily from 14th July to 9th September. Also open on weekends throughout the year and a number of other dates. Trains run from 10.30am to 4.30pm in the Summer and from 11.00am to 3.00pm in the Winter. Please contact the railway for further information.
Steam Working: No specific dates - trains may be Steam or diesel-hauled.
Prices: Adult Return £7.00   (Single £5.00)
Child Return £4.00   (Single £2.00)
Senior Citizen Return £6.00 (Single £4.00)
Family Ticket Return £16.00
(2 adults + 1 child)

Detailed Directions by Car:
From All Parts: Stanhope Station is located in Stanhope, just off the A689; Wolsingham Station is located in Wolsingham, also just off the A689.

WENSLEYDALE RAILWAY

Address: Leeming Bar Station, Leases Road, Leeming Bar, Northallerton DL7 9AR	**N° of Steam Locos:** Visiting loco in August
Telephone N°: 08454 50 54 74	**N° of Other Locos:** Various Diesel locos
Year Formed: The railway association was formed in 1990, the Railway PLC in 2000.	**N° of Members:** 3,500
Location of Line: Leeming Bar to Redmire	**Annual Membership Fee:** £12.00
Length of Line: Approximately 16 miles	**Approx N° of Visitors P.A.:** –
	Gauge: Standard
	Web site: www.wensleydalerailway.com

GENERAL INFORMATION

Nearest Mainline Station: Northallerton (4 miles)
Nearest Bus Station: Northallerton (4 miles)
Car & Coach Parking: Available at Leeming Bar, Leyburn and Redmire Stations
Souvenir Shop(s): Yes
Food & Drinks: Buffet carriages at Leeming Bar & Leyburn stations.

SPECIAL INFORMATION

Most services are via DMU and travel to Leyburn & Redmire tourist destinations in the Wensleydale Valley. Other heritage diesel groups also use the line.

OPERATING INFORMATION

Opening Times: Weekends only during the Winter plus other days over Christmas New Year. Open daily during the summer. Contact the railway for details.
Steam Working: During August 2007.
Prices: Adult Day Rover £12.00
Child Day Rover £6.00
Senior Citizen Day Rover £10.00
Family Day Rover £30.00
Note: Single and return tickets cost less than Day Rovers. Prices may differ during steam working.

Detailed Directions by Car:
From All Parts: Exit the A1 at the Leeming Bar exit and take the A684 towards Northallerton. The station is on the left after about ¼ mile close to the road junction and after the traffic lights. By Bus: The Dales & District 73 bus route travels between Northallerton and Leeming Bar.

WEST SOMERSET RAILWAY

Address: The Railway Station, Minehead, Somerset TA24 5BG	**Nº of Steam Locos**: 9
Telephone Nº: (01643) 704996 (enquiries)	**Nº of Other Locos**: 13
Year Formed: 1976	**Nº of Members**: 4,000
Location of Line: Bishops Lydeard (near Taunton) to Minehead	**Annual Membership Fee**: £15.00
Length of Line: 19¾ miles	**Approx Nº of Visitors P.A.**: 200,000
	Gauge: Standard
	Web site: www.west-somerset-railway.co.uk

GENERAL INFORMATION

Nearest Mainline Station: Taunton (4 miles)
Nearest Bus Station: Taunton (4½ miles) – Services 28 and 28A run to Bishops Lydeard. A free bus service runs from Taunton Railway Station and Silk Mills Park and Ride.
Car Parking: Free parking at Bishops Lydeard; Council car parking at Minehead
Coach Parking: As above
Souvenir Shop(s): Yes – at Minehead, Bishops Lydeard and Washford
Food & Drinks: Yes – At some stations. Buffet and Dining cars on all trains.

SPECIAL INFORMATION

Britain's longest Heritage railway runs through the Quantock Hills & along Bristol Channel Coast. Ten Stations with museums at Washford & Blue Anchor.

OPERATING INFORMATION

Opening Times: Various dates from March to December including daily from 22nd May to 3rd October. Open 9.30am to 5.30pm. Please contact the railway for more detailed dates.
Steam Working: All operating days except for during Diesel Galas.
Prices: Adult £13.00
Child £6.50
Family £32.70 (2 adults + 4 children)
Senior Citizen £11.60

Detailed Directions by Car:
Exit the M5 at Taunton (Junction 25) and follow signs for A358 to Williton and then the A39 for Minehead. In Minehead, brown tourist signs give directions to the railway.

OTHER RAILWAYS UNDER DEVELOPMENT

NORTHAMPTONSHIRE IRONSTONE RAILWAY TRUST

Hunsbury Hill Country Park
Camp Hill
Northampton
Telephone: (01604) 702031
Web site: www.nirt.co.uk
Year formed: 1974
Location of Line: Hunsbury Hill Country Park, near junction 15A of the M1
Length of Line: 1½ miles (when work has been completed)

The line is currently closed for engineering work. Members of the NIRT have been working for some time re-grading the line and re-laying track and are making good progress.

ROTHER VALLEY RAILWAY

Robertsbridge Station
Station Road
Robertsbridge
TN23 5DG
Telephone: (01580) 881833
Web site: www.rvr.org.uk
Year formed: 1997
Location of Line: Opposite Robertsbridge Mainline Railway Station

The ultimate aim of the railway is to reconnect Robertsbridge with Bodiam, providing a link to the main line for the Kent & East Sussex Railway. This would boost tourism in the Rother Valley area and help to relieve traffic congestion and pollution. Passengers would once again be able to link with mainline trains and visit Bodiam Castle and Tenterden without using their cars.

The completion of this plan is still some way off and at present volunteers are working on Phase 1 of the project which aims to introduce a diesel-hauled Brake Van service over the 600 yards of existing track.

THE KEITH & DUFFTOWN RAILWAY

Address: Dufftown Station, Dufftown, Banffshire, AB55 4BA
Telephone Nº: (01340) 821181
Year Formed: 2000
Location of Line: Keith to Dufftown
Length of Line: 11 miles

Nº of Steam Locos: None at present
Nº of Other Locos: 3
Nº of Members: –
Annual Membership Fee: –
Approx Nº of Visitors P.A.: –
Gauge: Standard
Web site: www.keith-dufftown.org.uk

GENERAL INFORMATION

Nearest Mainline Station: Keith (½ mile)
Nearest Bus Station: Keith
Car Parking: Available at the Station
Coach Parking: Available at the Station
Souvenir Shop(s): Yes
Food & Drinks: Available

SPECIAL INFORMATION

The Keith and Dufftown Railway is an eleven mile line linking the World's Malt Whisky Capital, Dufftown, to the market town of Keith. The line, which was reopened by volunteers during 2000 and 2001, passes through some of Scotland's most picturesque scenery, with forest and farmland, lochs and glens, castles and distilleries.

OPERATING INFORMATION

Opening Times: Weekends from Easter until the end of September and also on Fridays in June, July and August. Trains depart Dufftown from either 11.00am or 11.25am until 3.50pm.
Steam Working: None at present.
Prices: Adult Return £9.50
　　　　 Child Return £4.50
　　　　 Senior Citizen Return £7.50
　　　　 Family Return £23.00
Note: Shorter journeys are cheaper.

Detailed Directions by Car:
Keith Town Station is located in Keith, on the A96 Aberdeen to Inverness Road; Dufftown Station is about 1 mile to the north of the Dufftown Town Centre just off the A941 road to Elgin.